THREE STRIKES

THREE STRIKES

Miners, Musicians, Salesgirls, and the
Fighting Spirit of Labor's Last Century

HOWARD ZINN

~~~~

DANA FRANK

~~~~

ROBIN D. G. KELLEY

BEACON PRESS
BOSTON

Beacon Press
25 Beacon Street
Boston, Massachusetts 02108-2892
www.beacon.org

Beacon Press books
are published under the auspices of
the Unitarian Universalist Association of Congregations.

05 04   6 5 4 3 2

This book is printed on acid-free paper that meets the uncoated paper
ANSI/NISO specifications for permanence as revised in 1992.

Composition by Wilsted & Taylor Publishing Services

Library of Congress Cataloging-in-Publication Data

Zinn, Howard.
Three strikes : miners, musicians, salesgirls, and the
fighting spirit of labor's last century /
Howard Zinn, Dana Frank, Robin D. G. Kelley.
p.   cm.
Includes bibliographical references.
ISBN 0-8070-5012-1 (cloth)
ISBN 0-8070-5013-x (pbk.)
1. Strikes and lockouts—United States—Case studies.
2. Labor movement—United States—History—20th century.
I. Frank, Dana.   II. Kelley, Robin D. G.   III. Title.
HD5324 .Z56 2001
331.892'973'09041—dc21   2001001135

IN MEMORY OF
Debra Bernhardt

Contents

THREE STRIKES

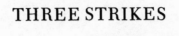

Introduction

Three Strikes is a critical tribute to labor's past and its most recent resurrection. In an age when production has become less pivotal to working-class life as capital flees the country in search of cheaper labor, relatively lower taxes, and a deregulated, frequently anti-union environment, the renewed labor movement has taken root in America's latest service-based economy. These "new workers" are concentrated in the healthcare professions, educational institutions, office building maintenance, telemarketing, food processing, food services and various retail establishments, and the prison-industrial complex. Among them we find more and more black and brown faces, increasingly more women than men (at least among the rank and file), and far too many folks cobbling together incomes from part-time work.

Faced with the challenges of "globalization," an increasingly diverse and mobile working class, and the shifting gender makeup of the nation's workforce, the most progressive labor leaders have extended their efforts beyond the workplace and beyond the boundaries of the nation-state. They reach out to the very communities where working people live, dream, and die, and in the process the union movement has been re-infused with the fighting spirit that working-class neighborhoods have nurtured for so long. The most visionary labor organizers are attempting to build a movement without borders, recognizing that any significant challenge to global capital depends on international solidarity.

Our tribute, as we have said, is a "critical" one. This book looks backward to look forward. It attempts to capture the fighting spirit of labor's last century, to see if there are any lessons for the struggles yet to come. But we are not interested in merely celebrating labor's heroic traditions of advocacy and resistance to exploitation. As each of the following strikes demonstrates, the struggles of American working people were far more complex, far more diverse, and far more interesting than common lore would have us believe.

There is a shameful failure in the history courses and texts of the American educational system to tell the truth about this dimension of the nation's history. The result is to deprive us all of the inspiring stories of diverse working people who fought against great odds—the combined power of business and government—to try to bring a measure of dignity to their lives. The strike Howard Zinn writes about for this book, the Colorado Coal Strike of 1913–14, is one of the most dramatic and violent examples of class conflict in American history. To bring it back into public view is to educate us all about an economic system which in its most essential character—the control of the lives of working people by powerful, invisible forces—has barely changed.

Today we are nearly overcome with the enormity of corporate power, now operating on a global stage. Yet young people, especially, are looking for new ways to challenge it. The story of the 1937 Woolworth's sit-down strike, told here by Dana Frank, resonates with the creative ideas and transnational targets of activists in the streets today. Woolworth's in the 1930s was the equivalent of Wal-Mart, the Gap, and K-Mart; it was also the subject of an enormous social movement against what people called "the chain store evil." In March of 1937, 108 very young white women (most of them were in their teens) suddenly occupied the largest Woolworth's in Detroit, Michigan, to demand a living wage and decent working conditions. Their raucous fun inside the store and the spectacular national solidarity outside are part of an uplifting tale of young people's visionary energy and, best of all, young women subverting the reigning stereotypes of the day about their relative interests in "boys," beautification, and economic betterment.

Our third strike story, told here by Robin Kelley, is about people who rarely thought of themselves as workers, a union waging an impossible war against technological displacement, the trials and tribulations of artists when the work of art, in this case music, is mass-produced, and the rapid transformation of the urban leisure industry and its impact on both cultural workers and working-class consumers. It is also about the limits of solidarity: What happens when the very technology used to destroy one segment of the work-force also generates new desires and pleasures for working people as a whole?

The questions raised by these stories are as timely in 2001 as they were in decades long past. The answers will invariably be different, but the great thing about history is that it stimulates our imaginations and casts light on our contemporary dilemmas as we discover how real people have dealt with similar circumstances. Their successes and failures, victories and missteps give us something to think about and to build upon.

Robin D. G. Kelley, Dana Frank, Howard Zinn
January 24, 2001

HOWARD ZINN

~~~~~

The Colorado Coal Strike, 1913–14

ON APRIL 21, 1914, in the quiet afternoon, a telephone linesman was making his way through the charred ruins of a miners' tent colony in southern Colorado. He lifted an iron cot covering a pit under one of the tents, and there he found the blackened, swollen bodies of eleven children and two women. The news was flashed swiftly to the world. The tragedy was given a name: the Ludlow Massacre.

Some Americans know about the Ludlow Massacre, though it does not appear in most of the history texts used in our schools and colleges. Woody Guthrie wrote a song about it, a dark, brooding song. But few know that the Ludlow Massacre was the central event in a fourteen-month strike of coal miners that took a toll of at least sixty-six lives—a strike which is one of the most dramatic and violent events in the history of this country.

Two governmental committees subsequently recorded over five thousand pages of firsthand testimony by participants in the Colorado coal strike. Thousands of newspaper stories and hundreds of magazine articles dealt with the conflict. Some of the most fascinating figures in American history were involved in some way in that event: Mother Jones and Eugene Debs, Woodrow Wilson, John D. Rockefeller and Ivy Lee, Upton Sinclair and John Reed.

Yet that story has been buried, in the way that labor struggles in general have been omitted or given brief mention in most mainstream accounts of the history of the United States. It deserves to be recalled, because embedded in the events of the Colorado strike are issues still alive today: the class struggle between owners of large enterprises and their workers, the special treatment of immigrant workers, the relationship between economic power and political power, the role of the press, and the way in which the culture censors out certain historical events.

The Colorado strike took place in a physical setting of vast proportions and staggering beauty. Down the center of the rectangle that is Colorado, from north to south, march an array of huge, breathtaking mountains—the Rockies—whose naked cliffs merge, on their eastern edge, with low hills covered with cedar and yellow pine. To the east of that is the plain—really a mile-high plateau—a tawny expanse of pasture grass sprinkled with prairie flowers in the spring and summer, and gleaming here and there with yellow-blossomed cactus.

Beneath the tremendous weight of the Rockies, in the course of countless centuries, decaying vegetation gradually mineralized into the black rock known as coal. The constantly increasing proportion of carbon in this rock transformed it from vegetable matter to peat, then to lignite and bituminous coal, and finally to anthracite.

Three great coalfields, consisting chiefly of bituminous coal, were formed in Colorado. One of them was contained within two counties in southern Colorado, Las Animas and Huerfano counties, just east of the mountains. This field was made up of about forty discontinuous seams, ranging from a few inches to fourteen feet thick. These seams were from two hundred and fifty to about five hundred feet deep.

The mining of these fields became possible on a large scale only in the 1870s, when the railroads moving west from Kansas City, south from Denver, and north from New Mexico, converged on the region. At about this time, settlers moving down the old Santa Fe trail built a town on the banks of the Purgatory River (*el Rio de las Animas Perdidas Purgatorio*—the river of lost souls), just east of the Sangre de Cristo (blood of Christ) mountains and about fifteen miles north of the New Mexican border.

The town was called Trinidad, and it became the center of the southern mining area. By 1913 it had about ten thousand people—miners, ranchers, farmers, and businessmen. From the main highways and railroad lines leading north out of Trinidad, branch railways and old wagon roads cut sharply west into the foothills of the mountains, into the steep-walled canyons where the mining camps lay. Scattered in these narrow canyons, on the flat bands of earth running along the canyon bottoms, were the huts of the miners, the mine buildings, and the mine entries.

It was a shocking contrast: the wild beauty of the Colorado countryside against the unspeakable squalor of these mining camps. The miners' huts, usually shared by several families, were made of clapboard walls and thin-planked floors, with leaking roofs, sagging doors, broken windows, and layers of old newspapers nailed to the walls to keep out the cold. Some families, particularly Negro families, were forced to live in tiny squares not much bigger than chicken coops.

Within sight of the huts were the coke ovens and the mine tipple, where coal was emptied from the cars that carried it to the surface. Thick clouds of soot clogged the air and settled on the ground, strangling any shoots of grass or flowers that tried to grow there. Wriggling along the canyon wall, behind the huts, was a now sluggish creek, dirty yellow and laden with the slag of the mine and the refuse of the camp. Alongside the creek the children played, barefoot, ragged, and often hungry.

Each mining camp was a feudal dominion, with the company acting as lord and master. Every camp had a marshal, a law enforcement officer paid by the company. The "laws" were the company's rules. Curfews were imposed, "suspicious" strangers were not allowed to visit the homes, the company store had a monopoly on goods sold in the camp. The doctor was a company doctor, the schoolteachers hired by the company.

In the early dawn, cages carried the men down into the blackness of the mine. There was usually a main tunnel, with dozens of branch tunnels leading into the "rooms," held up by timbers, where the miners hacked away at the face of the coal seam with hand picks and their helpers shoveled the coal into waiting railroad cars. The loaded cars were drawn along their tracks by mules to the main shaft, where they were lifted to the surface, and then to the top of the tipple, and then the coal showered down through the sorting screens into flatcars.

Since the average coal seam was about three feet high, the miners would often work on their knees or on their sides, never able to straighten up. The ventilation system was a crude affair that depended on the manipulation of tunnel doors by "trapper boys"—often thirteen or fourteen years old—who were being initiated into the work.

The first to labor in the Colorado Fuel & Iron Company's mines were Welshmen and Englishmen who had gained their experience in their mother countries. But with the great waves of immigration from southern Europe in the 1880s and 1890s, these were joined by Italians, Greeks, Poles, Hungarians, Montenegrins, and Serbs. There was also a large proportion of Mexicans and Negroes.

It was a man in charge of the "Sociological Department" of Colorado Fuel & Iron who described the mine bosses and camp officials this way: "At the bottom of the pit with pick and shovel the miner frequently found a grafting pit boss on his back. The camp superintendents as a whole impress me as most uncouth, ignorant, immoral, and in many instances the most brutal set of men that we have ever met. Blasphemous bullies."

Political power in Colorado rested in the hands of those who held economic power. This meant that the authority of Colorado

Fuel & Iron and the other mine operators was virtually supreme. A letter from company manager L. M. Bowers to the secretary of John D. Rockefeller Jr., written in May of 1913, describes the situation:

> The Colorado Fuel & Iron Company for many years was accused of being the political dictator of southern Colorado, and in fact was a mighty power in the whole state. When I came here it was said that the C. F. & I. voted every man and woman in their employ without any regard to their being naturalized or not; and even their mules, it used to be remarked, were registered, if they were fortunate enough to possess names. . . . The company became notorious in many sections for their support of the liquor interests. They established saloons everywhere they possibly could. . . . A sheriff, elected by the votes of the C. F. & I. Co. employees . . . established himself or became a partner in sixteen liquor stores in our coal mines.

The Colorado attorney general who conducted an investigation in Huerfano County in the fall of 1913, on the eve of the strike, said, "I found a very perfect political machine, just as much a machine as Tammany in New York." Another letter, from Superintendent Bowers to Rockefeller shortly after the strike began, describes the cooperation of the bankers and the governor against the strike, and refers to Governor Ammons (a Democrat and a supporter of President Woodrow Wilson) as "our little cowboy governor."

Colorado's deputy labor commissioner, Edwin Brake, later testified before the House Mines and Mining subcommittee that investigated the strike, "It's very seldom you can convict anyone in Huerfano County if he's got any friends. Jeff Farr, the sheriff, selects the jury and they're picked to convict or acquit as the case may be."

A Reverend Atkinson, who interviewed Governor Ammons during the strike, asked the governor if there was constitutional law and government in Colorado, to which Ammons replied, "Not a bit in those counties where the coal mines are located."

Company officials were appointed as election judges. Company-dominated coroners and judges prevented injured employees from collecting damages. Polling places were often on company property. J. C. Baldwin, gambler and bartender, was jury foreman in 80 percent of the cases tried in his county.

Much of the land on which these camps stood had been acquired under dubious circumstances under the provisions of the Desert Land Act, according to a report made in 1885 by the federal Land Commissioner.

In 1902, John D. Rockefeller Sr. bought control of the Colorado Fuel & Iron Corporation, the largest steel and coal producer in the West. The company produced 40 percent of the coal dug in Colorado. In 1911 he turned his interests in the corporation over to his son, John D. Rockefeller Jr., who decided major policy questions from his office at 26 Broadway in New York City. Actual management was handled in the Denver office of Jesse F. Welborn, chairman of the board of directors. By 1914 the company owned all the land in twenty-seven camps, including the houses, the saloons, the schools, the churches, and any other buildings within the camp environs.

From the very beginnings of the coal mine industry in Colorado, there was conflict between workers and management: an unsuccessful strike in 1876 (the very year Colorado was admitted to the Union), a successful strike in 1884 against a wage reduction. But the workday was still ten hours long, and in 1894 a strike for the eight-hour day failed.

The United Mine Workers of America was formed in 1890, "to unite in one organization, regardless of creed, color, or nationality, all workmen ... employed in and around coal mines." The first United Mine Workers local in Colorado was formed in 1900, and three years later there was an eleven-month strike, broken by strikebreakers and the National Guard. Some of those strikebreakers became the strikers of 1913.

The top leadership of the U.M.W. was often criticized by more militant elements of the labor movement as being too conservative.

The Colorado Coal Strike, 1913–14

And while it was the United Mine Workers who led the strike in 1913–14, members of two other organizations were on the scene and had varying degrees of influence over the miners. These were the I.W.W. (Industrial Workers of the World) and the Socialist Party, which had locals in Trinidad and other Colorado cities.

The I.W.W. was formed in Chicago, in June of 1905, as a trade union organization with a revolutionary goal. "The working class and the employing class have nothing in common" was the first sentence in its preamble. It reached the peak of its power in the successful Lawrence, Massachusetts, textile strike of 1912. During the period 1910–13, some 60,000 workers held membership cards at various times, but the influence of the organization was far greater than its numbers. It was an incessant prod to the regular trade unions for more militant action.

Despite the fact that many miners voted either Progressive (for Theodore Roosevelt) or Socialist (for Eugene Debs) in the presidential election of 1912, most of the United Mine Workers leadership, including the union officials in Colorado, supported the Democratic Party. The biographer of John Lawson, who represented the union in Colorado, New Mexico, and Utah, wrote, "John Lawson and his miners were naïve on the subject of politics. They invariably regarded the Democratic Party as the champion of the downtrodden, a position that could not have been sustained had they had the experience to draw obvious conclusions from the party's record in the state."

In December of 1912, Lawson reported to the national executive board of the union on the necessity of organizing the southern field. Lawson and Frank Hayes, vice president of the union, set up headquarters in Trinidad in early 1913. They asked Governor Ammons to arrange a conference with the mine operators. The operators refused. They would do nothing to indicate a recognition of the union. Lawson and Hayes sent out a letter addressed to all miners in southern Colorado:

Greetings. This is the day of your emancipation. This is the day when
liberty and progress come to abide in your midst. We call upon you this
day to enroll as a member of the greatest and most powerful labor organization in the world, the United Mine Workers of America.

Organizers worked quietly in pairs, one outside the mines, one
inside, and support for the union grew. Clandestine meetings were
held in the countryside; picnics became an occasion for enlisting
members. And on August 16, 1913, there took place the incident
that heated the atmosphere dramatically and inexorably led to the
strike. This was the shooting of Gerald Lippiatt, a thirty-two-year-
old Italian-American organizer for the United Mine Workers, on
the street in Trinidad.

There are many versions of what happened. The only details on
which all witnesses agreed were that Lippiatt, who had just arrived
in town, had walked down Commercial Street on a busy, noisy Saturday night; that he had encountered George Belcher and Walter
Belk, of the Baldwin-Felts Detective Agency and exchanged gunfire with Belcher; that Lippiatt had gotten off a shot that wounded
Belcher in the leg; and that eight shots were fired at Lippiatt, four of
which struck him. He died instantly.

Belcher and Belk were released on $10,000 bond. A coroner's
jury was formed of six Trinidad businessmen: the manager of the
Wells-Fargo Express company, the cashier of the Trinidad National
Bank, the president of the Sherman-Cosmer Mercantile Company,
the manager of the Columbia Hotel, the proprietor of a chain
of mercantile stores, and John C. Baldwin, gambler and saloon
keeper, who acted as foreman.

The jury was told by William Daselli, a miner, that he had witnessed the shooting and had been the first to reach Lippiatt. Daselli
said that Belk reached for his gun, Belcher pulled his gun and fired,
and Lippiatt fell, then fired from the ground. The jury decided that
it was a case of justifiable homicide.

Two days later, the scheduled convention of the State Federation
of Labor took place in Trinidad. An empty chair, draped in black,

represented Lippiatt, and feeling ran high against the Baldwin-Felts Agency and against the mine operators, who had hired the agency in preparation for possible labor trouble.

Frank Hayes, tall and powerfully built, with flaming red hair, and considered one of the few really militant officials of the United Mine Workers board, addressed the convention:

> If the Colorado mine owners, who have no regard for the miners union, could stand at the mouth of his mine some day when the black and swollen bodies of scores of his workmen are brought to the surface, as happened at Primero and other places in this state, and could hear the agonized cries of some mother, wife or child piteously begging that their loves ones be saved . . . they might then agree . . . that the miners union is justified in its demand for recognition.

On August 22 the delegates left the convention. Riding northward with them on the train was the coffin of Gerald Lippiatt. At Colorado Springs, Lippiatt was buried while a crowd of miners stood with heads bowed in the shadow of Pike's Peak and Lippiatt's fiancée wept quietly.

A letter from the U.M.W. policy committee was sent to fifty operators in southern Colorado asking for a conference. No reply came. Another letter invited the operators to a miners' convention to be held in Trinidad in mid-September. Again no reply.

Meanwhile, organizing was going on at a rapid rate. Miners from all the coal canyons in southern Colorado were being signed up as union members. Secret meetings were held in churches, at picnics, in abandoned workings hidden in the mountains. At hundreds of meetings, delegates were elected to represent the coal camps at the Trinidad convention.

At the same time, the mine operators were not idle. The Baldwin-Felts Agency began importing hundreds of men from the saloons and barrel-houses of Denver, and from points outside the state, to help break the impending strike. In Huerfano County, by the first of September, 326 men had been deputized by Sheriff Jeff Farr, all armed and paid by the coal companies.

On Monday, September 15, 1913, there was a parade of miners through the streets of Trinidad, and then the largest labor convention in Colorado history began its sessions. Two hundred and eighty delegates, representing every mine in Colorado as well as some in New Mexico and Utah, sat in the great opera house and sweated in the late summer heat.

For two days the convention's Scale and Policy Committee listened to the complaints of rank-and-file miners, who reported that they were being cheated to the tune of 400–800 pounds on each ton of coal; that the law allowing miners to elect checkweighmen of their own choice was being completely ignored; that they were paid in script worth ninety cents on the dollar (a violation of Colorado law); that the promise of an eight-hour day made by Colorado Fuel & Iron earlier that year had been ignored; that their wages could only be spent in company stores and saloons, where prices were from 25 to 40 percent higher; that they were forced to vote according to the wishes of the mine superintendent; that they were beaten and discharged for voicing complaints; and that armed guards conducted a reign of terror that kept the miners in subjection to the company.

A set of demands was adopted: recognition of the union was key, followed by the eight-hour day, wage increases, pay for "dead work" (laying tracks, shoring up the roof, etc.), elected checkweighmen, free choice of stores, boarding houses, and doctors, and the abolition of the guard system.

The operators claimed that the miners earned $20 a week, but the Colorado Bureau of Labor Statistics put their average take-home pay at $1.68 a day.

Perhaps what aroused the miners to rebellion more than anything was the refusal of the mine operators to spend money to insure the safety of the men as they worked hundreds of feet below the surface. There had been deadly explosions in the southern Colorado mines again and again. There were two primary causes for mine disasters: rotten timbers holding up the roofs of the caverns where the miners dug their coal, and the accumulation of gas and dust in dry conditions under which the gas ignited easily.

The Colorado Fuel & Iron Company's Primero mine was sprinkled only when the dust became thick enough to prevent the passage of the mules. The miners had a saying that the operators would "rather kill a man than maim a mule." In 1907 an explosion at Primero had killed twenty-four men; three years later another explosion had killed seventy-nine. In response, Colorado Fuel & Iron official L. M. Bowers said that such accidents "will happen and we have to make the best of it. . . . Work will be resumed as soon as the miners get over the excitement."

In 1910 the Starkville mine, where the state labor commissioner had previously reported a failure to sprinkle, suffered a frightful explosion. Forty miners were killed; rescuers were kept out of the mine during daylight hours so as not to cause panic. A spokesman for Colorado Fuel & Iron insisted Starkville was nongaseous. Four weeks later, a mine at Delagua, this one belonging to the Victor-American company, also exploded, killing eighty-two.

By the time the labor convention took place in Trinidad on September 15, 1913, the grievances had accumulated. When Mother Jones dramatically appeared to address the delegates, they were ready to be aroused.

Mary Jones, whom the miners came to call Mother, was born Mary Harris in Ireland, where as a child she had seen British troops march through the streets with the heads of Irishmen stuck on their bayonets, and where her grandfather had been hanged during the fight for Irish freedom. Her family had emigrated to Canada, and Mary, then in her twenties, moved to Michigan and then to Memphis, working as a dressmaker and a schoolteacher. At thirty-one, she married an ironworker named George Jones, and they had four children.

In 1867, a yellow fever epidemic struck Memphis. All of Mary Jones's children and her husband died. At the age of thirty-seven she left for Chicago, where she worked as a seamstress, later recalling, "Often while sewing for the lords and barons who lived in magnificent houses on the Lake Shore Drive, I would look out of the plate glass windows and see the poor, shivering wretches, jobless and hungry, walking alongside the frozen lake front."

She began attending meetings of the Knights of Labor, then the only national union that admitted women, and in the 1890s began organizing for the United Mine Workers. In 1903, with 100,000 miners on strike in Pennsylvania, including 16,000 children under age sixteen, she led a group of children on a twenty-two-day march to New York to confront President Theodore Roosevelt at his Oyster Bay home. She never found him there, but on the way she spoke at meetings of working people about child labor. In her autobiography she describes one of those meetings, near the Philadelphia city hall: "I put the little boys with their fingers off and hands crushed and maimed on a platform. I held up their mutilated hands and showed them to the crowd and made the statement that Philadelphia's mansions were built on the broken bones, the quivering hearts and drooping heads of these children."

Mother Jones was scathing in her denunciation of politicians, like the congressmen who passed legislation on behalf of the railroads but did nothing for working people. "I asked a man in prison once how he happened to get there. He had stolen a pair of shoes. I told him if he had stolen a railroad he could be a United States Senator." She was equally scornful of union leaders who compromised with employers, like United Mine Workers president John Mitchell. In her autobiography she wrote, "Mr. Mitchell died a rich man, distrusted by the working people whom he once served."

When the Colorado strike began, Mother Jones had just come from the coalfields of West Virginia. "Medieval West Virginia!" she called it later. "With its tent colonies on the bleak hills! With its grim men and women! When I get to the other side, I shall tell God Almighty about West Virginia!"

The Colorado Coal Strike, 1913–14

She stood on the platform in Trinidad that September of 1913 in a prim black dress embroidered with white lace, wisps of silvery hair curling around her forehead, a black bonnet on her head. She was five feet tall and weighed a hundred pounds. She addressed the delegates: "The question that arises today in the nation is an industrial oligarchy. . . . What would the coal in these mines and in these hills be worth unless you put your strength and muscle in to bring [it out]?"

She was an immigrant and had an instinctive understanding of the feelings of workers who had come from Italy, Poland, Greece, and other countries of southern and eastern Europe:

> A reporter for a Pittsburgh paper was once out here and was speaking to a manager of one of the C. F. & I. mines. He asked why the place was not propped safely and the manager humanely replied: "Oh damn it, dagos are cheaper than props." I want to say there are no dagos in this country! It has been the game that has been played down the history of the ruling class to divide the working class.

Mother Jones had been on the platform in 1905 when the radical Industrial Workers of the World was formed. She had written articles for the *International Socialist Review.* But her revolutionary spirit was uniquely her own, and she gave no unconditional loyalty to any organization. She began by telling the Colorado workers about West Virginia.

> Three thousand men assembled in Charlestown and we marched up with banners . . . and we walked into the state house grounds, for they are ours, and we have a right to take possession of them if we want to. . . . Now don't get on your knees. We have got no kings in America. Stand on both your feet with your head erect, said I, and present that document to the governor. . . . Don't wait, and don't say your honor, said I, because very few of those fellows have any honor and didn't know what it is! . . .
> Sure we'll get in the bull pen. There is nothing about that. I was in jail. God Almighty, what if you do, you built the jail! I was jailed . . . and tried in Federal court and the old judge said: "Did you read my injunc-

tion?" I said I did. "Did you notice that that injunction told you not to look at the mines and did you look at them?" "Certainly," I said. "Why did you do it?" the judge said. "Because there was a judge bigger than you, and he gave me my eyesight, and I am going to look at whatever I want to."

The convention exploded with laughter and applause, and then grew quiet as Mother Jones said, "You have . . . created more wealth than they in a thousand years of the Roman Republic, and yet you have not any. . . . When I get Colorado, Kansas and Alabama organized, I will tell God Almighty to take me to my rest. But not until then!"

The convention voted unanimously to strike on September 23, and both sides intensified their preparations. The coal operators, under the leadership of Colorado Fuel & Iron, met at Colorado Springs, deciding to stand together and resist the union's demands.

With evictions of miners from the mining camps quickly under way, the U.M.W. leased land just outside the bounds of company property and ordered tents. Funds were made available by the union to meet the needs of the strikers.

On the day of the walkout 11,000 miners, about 90 percent of the workforce, gathered up their belongings and left their homes in the camps. As they did so, rain began to fall, turning to sleet and snow, but it did not stop the procession of pushcarts and mule wagons, piled high with furniture and personal possessions and tiny children. Wheels sank through the ice into the mud, but they moved on. A reporter for the *Denver Express* called it "an exodus of woe, of a people leaving known fears for new terrors, a hopeless people seeking new hope, a people born to suffering going forth to new suffering."

Mother Jones later recalled that twenty-eight wagon loads of personal belongings came into the Ludlow colony alone that day, on roads deep in mud, with the horses weary and mothers carrying tiny babies in their arms. Tents and mattresses were wet, and the children had to sleep on those mattresses that night.

The Colorado Coal Strike, 1913–14

A thousand additional tents that had supposedly been shipped from West Virginia had not arrived, and so in this colony and others many families huddled beneath makeshift shelters or under their wagons. Snow continued to fall for two days, and one observer wrote that "the elements seemed to be in league with the operators." It took four days before the tents arrived. By then the sun had appeared, the snows had melted, sanitary trenches and storage pits had been dug, stoves installed, tent floors timbered.

Ludlow was the largest miners' colony, set up at a railroad depot eighteen miles north of Trinidad on a direct line to Walsenburg, at the edge of Colorado Fuel & Iron property. Near the Ludlow depot there were a Greek bakery, a few saloons, a post office, a few stores. There were four hundred tents here, for a thousand people, over a quarter of whom were children. In the course of the strike, twenty-one babies were born in these tents.

At Ludlow a wooden stage was built for meetings, and a large tent was set up for use as a school and as a kind of community center. Committees were elected to arrange for sanitation and entertainment. Miners' colonies were also set up at Aguilar, Forbes, Sopris, Segundo, and Walsenburg.

The Ludlow encampment was described later by Major Edward Boughton, who was adjutant-general of the Colorado National Guard: "The colony numbered hundreds of people of whom only a few families were Americans. The rest were for the most part Greeks, Montenegrins, Bulgars, Servians, Italians, Mexicans, Tyroleans, Croatians, Austrians, Savoyards, and other aliens from the Southern countries of Europe." Twenty-two different languages were spoken in the colony.

Violence between strikers and company men began almost immediately, and it can't be said with certainty which side committed the first act. Throughout the months of the strike, acts of violence by one side were met with retaliation from the other. But surely it was not an even match. Miners with rifles were arrayed against not only the machine guns of the Baldwin-Felts operatives but also the power of the state and its enforcers of "law and order." By the end of the strike, most of those dead and injured were miners and their families.

Near the Segundo railroad depot, five Greek strikers were doing some sabotage on a company-built footbridge across the Purgatory River when Bob Lee, chief guard at the Segundo coking plants and now a deputy sheriff, arrived. Lee was known to both miners and mine guards as a bully who victimized miners' wives as well as their husbands. Lee was on horseback, and as he rode towards the Greeks at the bridge he drew a rifle from the scabbard at the side of his saddle; but one of the Greeks fired first, the buckshot tearing into Lee's throat, killing him instantly.

The newly established U.S. Department of Labor tried to mediate between the U.M.W. and the mining operators, but the manager of Colorado Fuel & Iron, L. M. Bowers, distrusted the mediator, and wrote to Rockefeller that the companies would stand firm against the union until "our bones were bleached as white as chalk in these Rocky Mountains." Rockefeller replied that he agreed with this position. "Whatever the outcome we will stand by you to the end."

The Baldwin-Felts Agency constructed a special auto with a Gatling gun mounted on top, which became known as the Death Special. This auto, its sides armored, roamed the countryside with several agents carrying rifles in the front seat. On October 17, the Death Special attacked the tent colony at Forbes, killing one man and wounding two. A ten-year-old boy was left with nine bullets in his leg. In his book *Buried Unsung*, Zeese Papanikolas writes, "If there is anything that can account for the unconditional hatred the strikers would later show for the guards, for the panic that would sweep through those tents in waves throughout the rest of the strike, it is Forbes."

Meanwhile, hundreds of strikebreakers came into the area in a steady stream. They were deputized and paid $3.50 a day plus expenses. Wholesale arrests began. The sight of strikebreakers coming into the canyons aroused the strikers to fury. When they were intercepted, they were manhandled, once by a crowd of miners' wives and children. Buildings at the Primrose mine were dynamited. A gun battle took place between seventeen mounted mine guards and a group of strikers near the Ludlow colony. The operators told Governor Ammons that they had been attacked by "forty Greek and Montenegrin sharpshooters from the Balkan war."

Wholesale arrests of strikers continued. A few weeks after the start of the strike, forty-nine miners were marched to Trinidad between two rows of armed guards, with the Death Special crawling along to the rear, its guns trained on the strikers' backs. As the procession neared town, G. E. Jones, a member of the Western Federation of Miners, one of the founding unions of the I.W.W., tried to photograph the armed car. Albert C. Felts, manager of the Baldwin-Felts Agency, beat him senseless with the butt of his pistol while the deputies' rifles were trained on the man's body; then Jones was arrested for disturbing the peace.

Bowers reported to Rockefeller, "We are on top of a volcano. When men such as these [Department of Labor mediators], together with the cheap college professors and still cheaper writers in muck-raking magazines, supplemented by a lot of milk-and-water preachers . . . are permitted to assault the businessmen who have built up the great industries . . . it is time that vigorous measures are taken to put a stop to these vicious teachings."

Bowers also pointed to the threat to company's profits: "Our net earnings would have been the largest in the history of the company by $200,000, but for the increase in wages paid the employees during the last few months. . . . It is mighty discouraging to have this vicious gang come into our state and not only destroy our profit but eat into that which has heretofore been saved."

On October 26, a steel-clad train manned by 190 guards with machine guns and rifles headed for the Ludlow colony. It was intercepted by a detachment of armed miners and turned back after a pitched battle in which one mine guard was killed. The *New York Times* reported, "The situation is extremely critical tonight. More than 700 armed strikers are reported to be in the field against the mine guards." The use of the word "reported" suggested that the number had been exaggerated.

By the end of October there had been at least four battles between strikers and guards, and at least nine men had been killed. On October 28, Governor Ammons declared martial law. He also issued an order forbidding the import of strikebreakers from outside the state, but this was largely ignored.

The tent colonies were now in a state of siege, with machine guns and high-powered searchlights perched above them on inaccessible ridges, constantly aimed at the tents. The miners protested that their families could not sleep because of the glare, and the operators replied that if this was true they could pitch their tents farther from the coal properties.

Both sides were accumulating guns. Ethelbert Stewart, the Department of Labor's emissary and a man sympathetic to the miners, wrote to Washington, "If Caliban learns his master's language and uses it to curse him, the blame can not be all Caliban's. For Caliban will and must learn something, and the only language common to all, and which all understand in southern Colorado, is the voice of the gun."

On October 29, 1913, Governor Ammons ordered General John Chase, of the Colorado National Guard, to move his troops into the strike area. Chase was a Denver ophthalmologist, a gentleman farmer, and a church organist, but when he put on his National Guard uniform he saw himself in noble battle with socialists and anarchists. He had missed serving in the Spanish American War and had dreams of military grandeur. The pressures on the governor to call out the Guard are spelled out in a letter from L. M. Bowers to Rockefeller's New York office: "You will be interested to know that we have been able to secure the cooperation of all the bankers of the city, who have had three or four interviews with our little cowboy governor, agreeing to back the State and lend it all funds necessary to maintain the militia and afford ample protection so our miners could return to work."

Bowers's letter reveals a fundamental truth about labor struggles in American history—that powerful corporations have almost always found useful allies in the government and the press: "Besides the bankers, the chamber of commerce, the real estate exchange, together with a great many of the best business men, have been urging the governor to take steps to drive these vicious agitators out of the state. Another mighty power has been rounded up on behalf of the operators by the getting together of fourteen of the editors of the most important newspapers in the state."

The Colorado National Guard, under General Chase's command, consisted of two cavalry troops, two incomplete infantry regiments, one detachment of field artillery, a hospital corps, and a signal corps. The Guard had 14 horses at first, but bought 279 more; the mine owners paid for the keep of the horses. Six autos were used, two paid for by the operators. The enlisted personnel, according to an official report of the Adjutant-General's Office of Colorado, were mostly "small property-owners, clerks, professional men, farmers." There were about a thousand soldiers under Chase's command, although two thousand persons were on duty in the strike zone at various times.

The miners, having faced in the first five weeks of the strike what they considered a reign of terror at the hands of the private guards, now looked forward to the National Guard to "restore order." They did not know that the governor was sending these troops under pressure from the mine operators.

On the day before the Guard was due to arrive, several hundred miners camped at Ludlow put together their pennies and nickels to buy a large American flag, which flew the next morning over one of the strangest sights in Colorado history. Stretching for a mile along the road, from the tents of the Ludlow colony to the depot of the Colorado and Southern Railroad, were a thousand men, women, and children. They had been starving slowly for the past month, and it showed in their gaunt faces, their tired bodies. But they were dressed in their Sunday best, the miners' children decked out in white, all waving little American flags, and shouting shrill welcomes in English, Greek, Italian, and a dozen other tongues. A newly improvised and pitifully discordant band, dressed in faded but still colorful Greek and Serbian army uniforms, played "The Union Forever."

From the railway station came the first troop of cavalry, led by General Chase himself on a prancing white stallion. In the dust kicked up by the horses' hooves rumbled a small detachment of field artillery. Then two regiments of infantrymen, marching precisely, in wide-brimmed hats and yellow leggings. They were commanded by Lieutenant Linderfelt, a stocky veteran of other wars. Men, women, and children shouted and sang until the last contingent had disappeared past the tent colony, down Berwind Canyon.

But soon the same people who had wept with relief at the sight of the National Guard were bitterly mourning their dead and praying for deliverance from what they called "cavemen dressed in khaki."

In the last months of 1913, a committee was set up by the State Federation of Labor to respond to a challenge from the governor to prove accusations of brutality against the Guard. The committee was headed by Professor James Brewster, of the University of Colorado law school. It heard from 163 witnesses, the testimony filling 760 typewritten pages, telling of soldiers assaulting women and children and torturing prisoners. The National Guard made 172 arrests that winter. Among the incidents described in the Brewster report were the following:

Mary Thomas, a Welsh woman, mother of two, five feet tall with long red hair, was held for three weeks in a vermin-ridden cell.

One of the arrested strikers was forced to sleep on an icy cement floor. He died after twenty-five days.

The Colorado Coal Strike, 1913–14

A nineteen-year-old girl, pregnant, was dragged through an alley by guardsmen in the night until she lost consciousness.

Mrs. Yankinski, a miner's wife, was at home with her four children when militiamen broke in and stole her money. Before they left, one kicked her little girl in the face, breaking her nose.

In the town of Segundo, a group of drunken guardsmen forced a group of children to march about the city for two hours, prodding them with bayonets to keep them moving.

Marco Zeni, a miner, was forced to stay awake in his cell for five days by soldiers who threw water in his face and jabbed him continually with bayonets.

A teen-age boy who had welcomed the National Guard, who had waved and sang as Lieutenant Karl Linderfelt led his infantry troops past the tents, was later attacked by the powerfully built officer, who came across the boy on a road near the strikers' colony and knocked him unconscious with his fists. At another point the lieutenant told a miner, "I am Jesus Christ, and my men on horses are Jesus Christs—and we must be obeyed."

Karl Linderfelt, who was to become known for his viciousness in the course of the strike, had served in the Philippine War of 1900–1901, a war in which Filipino civilians, including women and children, had been massacred. In many ways the Philippine War resembles the later war in Vietnam—with atrocities committed by American soldiers, "search and destroy" missions, the dismemberment of enemy dead. Linderfelt had served in the Northern Luzon area of the Philippines, where few prisoners were taken and villages were burned.

Lieutenant Linderfelt held a special hatred for one striker, Louis Tikas, the leader of the Ludlow colony. Tikas was twenty-seven years old when the strike began. He had arrived in the United States from Greece when he was twenty, just at the time when the owners of the steel mills and mines of the West, who had been importing black labor from the South, decided it would be more profitable to hire recently arrived immigrants, like the Greeks, who might be intimidated by their new surroundings and would work for less.

Lou Tikas had had the benefit of a college education in Greece, and he was held in great affection by the miners. He was close to them in a way that John Lawson and other union officials could not be. One day at the end of November 1913, Lieutenant Linderfelt found Tikas alone and unarmed, beat him brutally, and had him dragged off to jail. John Lawson wired Governor Ammons: "We have reason to believe that it is Linderfelt's deliberate purpose to provoke the strikers to bloodshed. He has threatened to kill Louis Tikas."

In December of 1913, Lou Tikas and fifteen other prisoners of the Guard, among them Louis King, a black striker, lay in an ice-cold jail cell in Trinidad, with no charges yet brought against them. At this very time, Rockefeller was writing to his manager Bowers, "You are fighting a good fight, which is not only in the interest of your own company, but of other companies of Colorado and of the business interests of the entire country and of the laboring classes, quite as much."

One of the prisoners held with Tikas was another union organizer, Mike Livoda. Livoda was a Croatian who had come to America in 1903, worked in the Ohio steel mills, then headed west to the Colorado mines, where he became a U.M.W. organizer for three and a half dollars a day and expenses.

A month after Livoda arrived in Colorado, he had been taken into custody by four men who brought him to Jeff Farr, the notorious sheriff of Huerfano County. Farr asked his men, "Is that the son of a bitch?" He then told Livoda, "I'm king of this county. And if you want to do any of your dirty work you'll have to do it in Las Animas, not here." Livoda was put out on the railroad tracks and told to start walking. When he showed up in Huerfano County again, he was beaten, warned to get out of Colorado, and sent on his way. He walked for four hours into Walsenburg, where he found refuge in the shop of a Jewish tailor. Then he continued his work.

On December 15, 1913, Livoda, Tikas, and the other prisoners were released from jail. Livoda said later, "You know, when a fellow is fighting for something good he doesn't mind, even if they send him to jail. That is how I felt while I was in that dark, stuffy cell, and I was so happy I just keeping singing union songs all the time."

All that fall, the miners had been committing acts of violence against company employees who remained on the job. In early November, strikebreaker Pedro Armijo was shot to death while passing near the tent colony at Aguilar, one of the largest towns in the mine area, inhabited mostly by union people. At about the same time, Herbert Smith, a mine clerk scabbing in a Colorado Fuel & Iron mine, was brutally beaten near Trinidad. Two days later, four mine guards were killed at Laved while escorting another scab.

That same month, George Belcher, the killer of U.M.W. organizer Gerald Lippiatt, was leaving a Trinidad drugstore and stopped on the corner to light a cigar. Hundreds of soldiers were in the square, plus fifty deputies and a number of detectives. As Belcher struck a match, a bullet from an unseen rifle entered the base of his brain, killing him instantly. Although several union men were arrested, no evidence was ever produced and the case went unsolved.

The miners were reacting not only to the killing of Lippiatt, which they had not forgotten, but also to the machine gun attacks on the tent colonies by the Baldwin-Felts agents, to the clandestine importation of strikebreakers, and to the depredations of the National Guard.

In the month of December 1913, Colorado experienced the worst snow seen in thirty years—forty-two inches fell on Denver. Colorado Fuel & Iron officials thought the storms might compel the miners to leave the tents for "the comfortable houses and employment at the mines," as they put it in one of their memos. But they did not understand the miners. And it was this lack of comprehension, and their frustration at the miners' refusal to surrender even under horrendous conditions, that led the mine operators to escalate their attempts to break the strike. The governor became their instrument.

Early in December, Governor Ammons rescinded his original order forbidding strikebreakers to come in from outside the state. It had been ignored in any event, but now that it had been withdrawn the National Guard openly protected the strikebreakers, escorting them to the mines.

The railroad junction of Ludlow became a battleground. Black men from the South and recent immigrants from the Balkans were brought in. Often they were not told that a strike was on. The trains carrying them into the district often had the blinds drawn, the doors locked. As they got off the train they were jeered by people from the Ludlow tent colony—men, women, children—who were lined up at the depot. When found alone, strikebreakers were often beaten.

There were other kinds of encounters. Three black strikebreakers were captured, given food in the Ludlow colony, then released. Another day, strikers intercepted several Greeks at the Walsenburg depot, took them to the house of a miner in Walsenburg, made them a meal, and convinced them to support the union. But when their host, Kostas Markos, took them into town, they were surrounded by militiamen. Markos, who was carrying a gun, was beaten and thrown into jail. The Greeks were forced into a mine.

Kostas Markos was kept on the damp cement floor of a cell in the basement of the Walsenburg courthouse for twenty-two days. He was ill with rheumatism, but no doctor came to see him. Shortly after his release from prison he died. Later testimony before a subcommittee of the House Mines and Mining Committee appointed to determine whether federal laws were being violated in respect to peonage disclosed that "Salvatore Valentin, a Sicilian, told the committee that he had been brought from Pittsburgh through deception and forced to work in the Delagua mine. One of his fellow strikebreakers, he said, was shot and killed in the mines by an unknown person."

Witnesses before the committee made dozens of accusations of peonage. Strikebreakers were deceived about the existence of a strike. At one point a contingent of workers from St. Louis disembarked from the train in Colorado and were surprised to find themselves "protected" by militiamen with unsheathed bayonets. At the end of January, fifty Bulgarians brought in to work at Tabasco Canyon who had been told there was no strike discovered otherwise. They evaded their guards and fled through the snow to the Ludlow colony, where Lou Tikas saw to it that they were fed, and, together with others who had made their way to Ludlow, brought into Trinidad to give affidavits to union attorneys.

Through all of this, the National Guard had its hands full trying to keep Mother Jones out of the strike area. General Chase had said, "She will be jailed immediately if she comes to Trinidad. I am not going to give her a chance to make any more speeches here. She is dangerous because she inflames the minds of the strikers."

On January 4, 1914, Mother Jones set out from Denver "to help my boys." She was then eighty-three years old. Arriving in Trinidad, she was immediately arrested and put on a train back to Denver. General Chase declared that if she returned to the strike zone she would be held incommunicado. She responded defiantly that she would return "when Colorado is made part of the United States." Speaking in Denver to union people she said, "I serve notice on the governor that this state doesn't belong to him—it belongs to the nation and I own a share of stock in it. Ammons or Chase either one can shoot me, but I will talk from the grave."

She left again for Trinidad on January 12, walking through the railroad yard to get on the train undetected by the detectives posted on the platform in the station. She got off at an unscheduled stop north of Trinidad, walked into town, and made her way to the Toltec Hotel. She spent three hours in her room, across the street from militia headquarters, before she was discovered. As a hundred and fifty militiamen surrounded the hotel, General Chase entered her room and took her into custody. She was taken to a hospital on the outskirts of Trinidad, where five guards kept a twenty-four-hour watch over her.

Mother Jones had been imprisoned for ten days when women began to arrive in Trinidad from all over the state, women who had heard her speak and been inspired. At one time she had told them,

> This earth was made for you, was it not? And it was here a long time before the Colorado Fuel & Iron came upon it. When the C. F. & I. came upon this earth they did not get a mortgage on it, did they? No they did not. The earth was here long before they came, and it will be here when their rotten carcasses burn up in hell. . . . You will be free. Poverty and misery will be unknown. We will turn the jails into playgrounds for the children. We will build homes, and not dog kennels and shacks as you have them now. . . . You men and women will have to stand and fight.

Now they gathered a thousand strong at the train station to protest the jailing of Mother Jones. With an Italian woman carrying the American flag at the head of the parade, they began to march through the town.

They soon found their path blocked by National Guard cavalrymen, sabers drawn, led personally by General Chase, who pranced back and forth on his horse before the first rank of guardsmen. Chase called on the women to turn back, but they would not. Chase found a sixteen-year-old girl, Sarah Slater, in his path, and when she did not respond to his command he kicked at her with his stirruped foot. His horse bolted and Chase fell onto the street as the women jeered.

The general got back on his horse and shouted to his troops, "Ride down the women!" The cavalrymen charged into the crowd, tearing banners and flags from the women's hands and swinging their sabers. Several women were slashed. A soldier brought his rifle butt down hard on Sarah Slater's toes. (General Chase said later that this was an effective method of mob control.)

The Colorado Coal Strike, 1913–14

Eighteen marchers were arrested. Mary Thomas, the diminutive Welsh mother of two, was not in the parade, but she had watched from the sidewalk and taunted the soldiers. She was dragged off and put in a cell along with her daughters, three and four years old. She told later how she sang to supporters gathered outside the jail until the police drove the crowd away. Mary Thomas and her children were kept in jail for three weeks.

Chase had so many prisoners by now that he set up a "military commission" to try the overload. The committee consisted of a Pueblo banker, a Denver physician, a manufacturer, an attorney, a businessman, and a Montrose real estate man. Major Edward Boughton, a Denver and Cripple Creek attorney, was made the commission's judge advocate.

Mother Jones was held incommunicado for ten weeks, with six soldiers guarding her day and night. She spoke later of having friendly conversations with some of them. Finally she was put on a train for Denver, guarded by a National Guard colonel.

The State Federation of Labor's Brewster committee, after hearing all the testimony about the brutality of the National Guard, addressed itself to the governor in early 1914: "We ask, sir, your solemn consideration of this question. How much longer will workingmen continue to follow the Stars and Stripes when they repeatedly see the principles for which the Stars and Stripes have stood contemptuously disregarded by those in whose hands, for a time, lies might without right?"

The committee recommended that General Chase either resign or be removed; that three of the Guard officers, including Lieutenant Linderfelt, be suspended; that the private guards paid by the coal operators be discharged; that no workers be brought in under deception. The governor followed none of the recommendations, saying that the committee had heard only one side. There was truth to this, since guardsmen had not been permitted to testify before the committee.

February and March of 1914 were cold months and quiet ones. Only occasionally could a burst of gunfire be heard in the hills. But hunger and freezing temperatures plagued the miners and their families. As Zeese Papanikolas describes it,

> Winter had hit hard at the people in the camps. . . . At Ludlow the paths worn between the tents and the privies or the coal piles or Snodgrass' little tin-sided store turned sludgy between the drifts of dirty snow or slicked over with ice. Water froze in the barrels outside the tents. When it stormed, gangs of men pulled the snow off the sagging tent roofs to keep them from crashing down. The men still went out with shovels and picks and a loop of wire looking for rabbits, but there were thirteen hundred mouths to feed in Ludlow alone and the game was getting pushed back deeper and deeper into the hills. The strike benefits never stretched far enough to fill the strikers' bellies. They were hungry in the camps, and they began to wear on one another. The women spent days huddled under their blankets with the children in the biting cold.

Papanikolas also observes, "In a certain subtle but elemental way the course of the strike had changed the real nature of the relations of women and men." The importance of the women in the family was never more evident. Not only were they out on the picket lines, often with their children, but they carried the coal and the water, did the cooking and the mending of clothes, held the families together.

As the strike wore on, the radical elements among the miners were active in maintaining morale, in bringing to the miners the larger implications of the strike—the class struggle going on in the United States and the world, the possibility of a better way of life. The Trinidad branch of the Socialist Party held meetings throughout the strike zone. A left-wing socialist, George Falconer, visited Colorado and reported that at a meeting of two hundred miners in Starkville, he and an Italian socialist named Amando Pelizzari were arrested. At Ludlow, over five hundred miners and their families gathered in the big tent to hear socialist speeches and take literature, while armed soldiers waited outside on the snow-clad plain. At a meeting in Aguilar, company soldiers surrounded the hall. In Walsenburg six hundred miners attended.

With the spring approaching, the mine operators began to listen to the incessant complaints of Governor Ammons. The state was heavily in debt to the bankers. Funds were running out for maintaining the National Guard. The payroll alone was $30,000 a month, and critics pointed to the disproportionate number of officers in the guard—397 officers to 695 privates. As the state grew less and less able to pay salaries, the regular enlisted militia began to drop out. Taking the places of many of these men, wearing the same uniforms, were the mine guards of Colorado Fuel & Iron, still drawing pay from the company.

In early April of 1914, without warning, Governor Ammons recalled the bulk of the Colorado National Guard. Only thirty-five men in Company B, mostly former mine guards, were left. On April 18, a hundred deputies in the pay of Colorado Fuel & Iron were formed into Troop A of the National Guard and sent to join Company B. The designated spot: a rocky ridge overlooking the thousand men, women, and children who lived in the tent colony at Ludlow.

The two officers selected to take charge were Major Pat Hamrock, a local saloon keeper, and a man well known to the residents of Ludlow, Lieutenant Karl Linderfelt. Linderfelt's men in Troop A, according to a report to the governor by Major Boughton, were "superintendents, foremen, the clerical force, physicians, storekeepers, mine guards, and other residents of the coal camps."

On April 19, 1914, Easter Sunday for the Greek Orthodox Church, a group of the Ludlow strikers were picnicking in a nearby meadow. It was one of the first sunny days of spring, and they were playing baseball. Over the hill from the north came five gunmen on horseback, rifles slung over their shoulders. They stopped near the players, and one of them shouted, "Have your fun today! We'll have our roast tomorrow."

On Monday morning, April 20, the Ludlow colonists were still sleeping in their tents when the quiet of dawn was shaken by a violent explosion. Rushing from their tents, the strikers could see columns of black smoke rising slowly to the sky from the hill where the militia were stationed. Major Hamrock had exploded two dynamite bombs as a signal.

For a little while the countryside was unbearably still and tense. Then, at exactly 9:00 A.M., the dull clatter of a machine gun began and the first bullets ripped through the canvas of the tents. The clatter became a deafening roar as more machine guns went into action. One of the people who died was Frank Snyder. He was ten years old. His father told about it afterward: "The boy Frank was sitting on the floor . . . and he was in the act of stooping to kiss or caress his sister. . . . I was standing near the front door of my tent and I heard the impact of the bullet striking the boy's head and the crack . . . as it exploded inside of his brain."

Mingling with the gunfire were the wild cries of women as they ran from tent to tent, hugging children to their breasts, seeking shelter. Some managed to run off into the hills and hide in nearby ranch houses. Others crawled into the dark pits and caves which had been dug under a few of the tents.

Meanwhile, men were dashing away from the encampment to draw off the fire. They flung themselves into deep arroyos—dried-up streambeds. Now the high-powered rifles of the militiamen joined in and poured a hail of explosive bullets into the tents and into the arroyos. This continued all through the morning and into the afternoon, while men, women, and children huddled wherever they had found shelter, without food or water. At 4:30 P.M. a train from Trinidad brought more guards—and more machine guns.

Eyewitness Frank Didano reported, "The firing of the machine guns was awful. They fired thousands and thousands of shots. There were very few guns in the tent colony. Not over fifty, including shotguns. Women and children were afraid to crawl out of the shallow pits under the tents. Several men were killed trying to get to them.

The Colorado Coal Strike, 1913–14

The soldiers and mine guards tried to kill everybody; anything they saw move, even a dog, they shot at." Didano's estimate of the number of guns in the colony may not have been accurate, but certainly the miners' weapons were no match for what was coming to them. (All through the strike the operators had tried to spread the idea, often abetted by the press, that the miners had stockpiled large stores of ammunition and dynamite.)

That afternoon, the man the miners loved, Lou Tikas, was in the big tent, caring for women and children and aiding the wounded, when a telephone, its wires amazingly intact, started ringing. It was Lieutenant Linderfelt, up on the hill. He wanted to see Tikas— it was urgent. Tikas refused, hung up. The phone rang insistently —again and again. Tikas reconsidered. Perhaps he could stop the murder. He answered the phone. He would come.

Carrying a white flag, Tikas met Linderfelt on the hill. The lieutenant was surrounded by militiamen. The two talked. Suddenly Linderfelt, his face contorted with rage, raised his rifle and brought the stock down with all his strength on Tikas's skull. The rifle broke in two as the strike leader fell to the ground.

Godfrey Irwin, a young electrical engineer visiting Colorado with a friend, accidentally witnessed the scene from a nearby cliff. He later described the next few moments for the *New York World*: "Tikas fell face downward. As he lay there, we saw the militiamen fall back. Then they aimed their rifles and fired into the unconscious man's body. It was the first murder I had ever seen."

Two other strikers, unarmed and under guard, met their deaths on the hill in a similar manner.

As the sun lowered gradually behind the black hills, soldiers moved slowly down into the dark shadows alongside the tents. They were drenching the canvas with coal oil. The tents caught fire in rapid succession. Godfrey Irwin wrote,

> We watched from our rock shelter while the militia dragged up their
> machine guns and poured a murderous fire into the arroyos from a

height by Water Tank Hill above the Ludlow depot. Then came the firing of the tents. I am positive that by no possible chance could they have been set ablaze accidentally. The militiamen were thick about the northern corner of the colony where the fire started, and we could see distinctly from our lofty observation place what looked like a blazing torch waved in the midst of the militia a few seconds before the general conflagration swept through the place.

While bullets whistled through the flaming canvas, people fled in panic from their tents and from the caves beneath. A dispatch to the *New York Times* read,

> A seven-year-old girl dashed from under a blazing tent and heard the scream of bullets about her ears. Insane from fright, she ran into a tent again and fell into the hole with the remainder of her family to die with them. The child is said to have been a daughter of Charles Costa, a union leader at Aguilar, who perished with his wife and another child. . . .
>
> James Fyler, financial secretary of the Trinidad local . . . died with a bullet in his forehead as he was attempting to rescue his wife from the flames. . . . Mrs. Marcelina Pedragon, her skirt ablaze, carried her youngest child from the flames, leaving two others behind.

And in another article the *Times* reported, "An unidentified man, driving a horse attached to a light buggy, dashed from the tents waving a white flag, just after the fire started. When ordered to halt he opened fire with a revolver and was killed by a return volley from the militia."

The tents became crackling torches, and for hours the countryside was aglow with a ghastly light while men, women, and children roamed like animals in the hills, seeking their loved ones. At 8:30 P.M. the militia "captured" the smoldering pile of ashes that now was Ludlow.

It was on the following day, April 21, that the bodies of the women and children were found in the pit beneath the tent.

The *New York Times* headline read, "WOMEN AND CHILDREN

The Colorado Coal Strike, 1913–14

ROASTED IN PITS OF TENT COLONY AS FLAMES DESTROY IT. MIN-
ERS STORE OF AMMUNITION AND DYNAMITE EXPLODED, SCAT-
TERING DEATH AND RUIN." It was clear that the tent colony had
been set aflame by the National Guard, but the paper was claiming,
as has so often happened, that it was the victims who were responsible for the disaster.

A seemingly endless stream of men and women filed past the
rows of coffins which filled the morgue in Trinidad. For Lou Tikas,
there was a separate funeral. Thousands stood in the streets and
wept. A few blocks from the morgue, in a windowless room in a
cheap boarding house, Mary Pedragon stared at the walls, her mind
gone. The two children she had not been able to carry had died in
the pit.

The *Rocky Mountain News*, heretofore a fairly conservative
newspaper, wrote,

> Out of this infamy one fact stands clear. Machine guns did the mur-
> der. . . . It was private war, with the wealth of the richest man in the
> world behind the armed guards. The blood of the women and chil-
> dren, burned and shot like rats, cries aloud from the ground. The great
> state of Colorado has failed them. It has betrayed them. Her militia,
> which should have been the impartial protectors of the peace, have
> acted as murderous gunmen. . . . Explosive bullets have been used on
> children. Does the bloodiest page in the French Revolution approach
> this in hideousness?

The *New York Times* adopted a somewhat different approach. It
seemed to be angry, not so much at the horrible acts that had been
perpetrated during the massacre, but at the fact that the militia and
the authorities had been stupid enough to create a situation on
which the strikers might capitalize to their advantage. A *Times* editorial read,

> Somebody blundered. Worse than the order that sent the Light Bri-
> gade into the jaws of death, worse in its effect than the Black Hole of
> Calcutta, was the order that trained the machine guns of the state mili-

tia of Colorado upon the strikers' camp at Ludlow, burned its tents, and suffocated to death the scores of women and children who had taken refuge in the rifle pits and trenches. . . . Strike organizers cannot escape full measure of blame for the labor war. . . . But no situation can justify the acts of a militia that compels women and babes to lie in ditches and cellars twenty four hours without food or water, exposes them to cannon and rifle fire, and lets them die like trapped animals in the flames of their camp. . . . [The workers] are now nerved to take this citadel [the doctrine of the right to work] by storm. They used violence against this doctrine. But when a sovereign State employs such horrible means, what may not be expected from the anarchy that ensues?

Funerals continued in Trinidad, and great memorial meetings. Families of the victims spoke and wept, and demanded redress, and the crowds wept with them.

Now a thousand miners turned from the coffins of the dead, took up their guns, and set out together for the back country. They were joined by union miners from a dozen neighboring camps, who left wives and children behind and swarmed over the hills, carrying arms and ammunition. They swept across the coal country, from Dalagua to Rouse, leaving in their wake the ashes of burned tipples, the rubble of dynamited mines, and the corpses of strikebreakers and militiamen.

Now, with the miners taking up arms against the militia, the *New York Times* editorialized, "With the deadliest weapons of civilization in the hands of savage-minded men, there can be no telling to what lengths the war in Colorado will go unless it is quelled by force. The President should turn his attention from Mexico long enough to take stern measures in Colorado."

The *Times* was referring to increasing tensions between Mexico and the United States, a situation that had been unfolding and came to a crisis point on the day of the massacre at Ludlow.

After taking half of Mexican territory in the Mexican War of

1846–48, the United States had remained strongly interested in the internal affairs of that country, as American investments, especially in Mexican oil, grew over the years. By 1913, these investments totaled a billion dollars, more than those of all other nations combined. William Randolph Hearst, in addition to his interest in oil, had inherited huge amounts of land in Mexico, and had become a powerful voice for U.S. interference in Mexican politics to protect these investments.

There was a new Mexican president in 1913, Victoriano Huerta, who had deposed his populist predecessor, Francisco Madero, in a bloody coup. President Woodrow Wilson refused to recognize Huerta, which was attributed by some observers to Wilson's abhorrence for dictatorship, by others to a desire for a more stable government that could preserve U.S. business interests. Wilson became more and more aggressive towards Huerta, demanding his resignation and allowing war materials to flow to Huerta's political opponents.

Wilson's language was the language of idealism ("Morality and not expediency is the thing that must guide us") but his actions were more in accord with the oil interests, one of whose spokesmen in the Senate declared, "I think those hearing me will live to see the Mexican border pushed to the Panama Canal." As the tension grew between Huerta and the United States, on April 9, 1914, the crew of an American naval vessel loading supplies at the Mexican port of Tampico was arrested, charged with violating martial law.

The sailors were released shortly, with an apology, but the commander of the American fleet demanded a formal apology, punishment of the responsible officer, and "that you publicly hoist the American flag in a prominent position on shore and salute it with twenty-one guns, which salute will be duly returned by this ship."

The Mexican foreign minister, Portillo y Rojas, announced that Mexico would exchange salutes with the United States, and would even salute first, but could not salute unconditionally. The officer who had arrested the American servicemen was under arrest, Rojas said, and the Americans had been freed even before an investigation. "Mexico has yielded as much as her dignity will permit. Mexico trusts to the fairmindedness and spirit of justice of the American people."

That trust turned out not to be justified. President Wilson declared that unless the Mexican president acted before 6 P.M. on Sunday, April 19, he would take the situation to Congress for further action. Meanwhile, 22,000 men and fifty-two ships were ready. It seemed that long before the Tampico incident, plans for intervention in Mexico had been prepared. The *Times* reported, "CAMPAIGN WORKED OUT BY NAVAL EXPERTS IN RECENT MONTHS NOW BEING CARRIED OUT IN DETAIL."

On April 20, Wilson sent a message to Congress asking for the right to use armed force: "There can in what we do be no thought of aggression or selfish aggrandizement. We seek to maintain the dignity and authority of the United States only because we wish always to keep our great influence unimpaired for the uses of liberty, both in the United States, and wherever else it may be employed for the benefit of mankind."

Wilson's idealistic words were typical of his presidency. In the next several years he would send American troops to occupy Haiti and the Dominican Republic, again claiming it was for "the uses of liberty . . . the benefit of mankind." In fact, U.S. business interests required stability in those countries, which could be guaranteed by the presence of American marines.

The *Times*, in its editorial on the Mexican situation, said,

> The President asked of Congress yesterday authority not to make war upon Mexico in the full sense of the word, but to apply coercive pressure to Huerta with intent to force his compliance with our just demands.
>
> Just as when we went to war with Spain there were those who insisted that we should ignore the destruction of the *Maine* . . . so there

are now those who hold that Huerta is in the right and that he has given us no cause of offense. As to that, we may trust the just mind, the sound judgment, and the peaceful temper of President Wilson.

There is not the slightest occasion for popular excitement over the Mexican affair; there is no reason why anybody should get nervous either about the stock market or about his business.

American naval guns then proceeded to bomb Vera Cruz, and ten boatloads of marines landed. Over a hundred Mexicans were killed, the press announced.

The feelings of one section of the population were clear. As the *Times* reported, "The five hundred or more business men who attended the luncheon of the Members Council of the Merchants Association of New York jumped to their feet yesterday when William C. Breed, the toastmaster, called upon those present to express their loyalty to President Wilson 'to whatever course he shall determine necessary to restore peace, order, and a stable government in the Republic of Mexico.'"

But the miners of Colorado, with their nation facing such a critical question, with National Guardsmen needed to patrol the borders of Mexico, took a dim view of the "police action" and of the calls upon their "patriotism." They were influenced in this by two factors: the horror they had just been through, inflicted upon them not by any foreign tyranny but by the private business interests and armed forces of their own government; and the ideology of the radical and antiwar movements in the United States.

Here was the radical viewpoint toward the Mexican situation, expressed in the socialist press and at meetings throughout the country: the United States had gone into Mexico to protect Rockefeller's oil and William Randolph Hearst's ranches: "The wars in Mexico and Colorado are both Standard Oil wars" (*International Socialist Review*, June 1914). We have no country, radicals said—all workers are our countrymen—the only foreigner is the capitalist. In this view, the former Mexican president, Porfirio Diaz, had favored British oil interests rather than Rockefeller's, Francisco Madero had been used by Rockefeller to regain control of Mexico's oil, and Wilson was a puppet of Rockefeller.

The Women's Peace Association in Denver said, "While Colorado is disgracing herself in the eyes of the world, the man who is responsible for the disgrace sits in his office in New York City. He is John D. Rockefeller, Jr." A meeting of women at Cooper Union in New York denounced Rockefeller and condemned the landing of troops at Vera Cruz. The New York executive committee of the Socialist Party asked Wilson to recall forces from Mexico and protect the Colorado miners.

A week after the Ludlow Massacre, a *Times* editorial hit out at two clergymen, the Reverend Percy Stickney Grant of Manhattan, and the Reverend John Howard Melish of Brooklyn, who had denounced from their pulpits the actions of the National Guard against the strikers. The *Times* said, "These are sympathetic utterances [the sermons of Grant and Melish] and differ from . . . cold impartiality. . . . There are those who think that infamy in Colorado consists in the fact that the militia are shooting workers. It may be contended that there is something like infamy in the opposition of workers to society and order. The militia are as impersonal and impartial as the law."

During this whole period, the *New York Times* published only one letter to the editor concerning the strike. It should be taken into consideration that any major event brings hundreds of letters to the newspapers, and that the selection of these letters reflects, in strong measure, editorial policy. This one letter was signed "W. C. C." and declared that John D. Rockefeller Jr. "is doing a patriotic duty. . . . He should have the approval of all who love justice and true freedom."

On April 22, a "Call to Arms" went out from Denver, addressed to "the Unionists of Colorado." The letter was signed by John Lawson,

John McLennon, Ed Doyle, and several other U.M.W. officials, as well as Ernest Mills, secretary-treasurer of the Western Federation of Miners. It read,

> Organize the men in your community in companies of volunteers to protect the workers of Colorado against the murder and cremation of men, women, and children by armed assassins in the employ of coal corporations, serving under the guise of state militiamen. . . .
>
> The state is furnishing no protection to us and we must protect ourselves, our wives and children, from these murderous assassins. We seek no quarrel with the state and we expect to break no law. We intend to exercise our lawful right as citizens to defend our homes and our constitutional rights.

Not until April 23 did the militia allow all the bodies to be removed from the Ludlow ruins. It was reported that in Trinidad "men throng the streets about the union headquarters and demand guns with which to work vengeances upon the militia, which they hold responsible for the destruction of their homes and the death of their women and children."

The press also reported fighting in an area of three square miles, bordered on the west by Berwind and Hastings, on the east by the Barnes station, on the north by the Ludlow tent colony, and on the south by Rameyville. The battlefield was isolated by the cutting of telephone and telegraph wires. The *New York Times* wrote, "MEN FROM OTHER UNION CAMPS JOIN FIGHTERS IN HILLS TO AVENGE THEIR SLAIN: The militia . . . are preparing for a machine-gun sortie. . . . On the surrounding hills, sheltered by rocks and boulders, four hundred strikers await their coming, while their ranks are being swelled by grim-faced men who tramped overland in the dark, carrying guns and ammunition from the neighboring union camps."

The Trinidad Red Cross issued a statement that twenty-six bodies of strikers had been found at Ludlow. There were conflicting reports as to how many had been killed.

Three hundred armed strikers marched from Fremont County tent colonies to aid the embattled miners of southern Colorado. Four train crews of the Colorado and Southern Railroad refused to take soldiers and ammunition from Trinidad to Ludlow. This action touched off talk of a general strike by the Brotherhood of Locomotive Engineers and Trainmen and the Colorado State Federation of Labor.

From coast to coast, people responded to the appeal of the Colorado miners. Hundreds of mass meetings were held. Thousands of dollars were sent for arms and ammunition. Conservative unions as far away as Philadelphia took action.

While various groups called for federal intervention to restore law and order, Rockefeller sent a telegram to Congress saying that mining company officials were the "only ones competent to deal with the questions." A telegram to President Wilson from twenty "independent" coal operators in Colorado declared that "we heartily endorse" the Colorado Fuel & Iron position. Meanwhile, John P. White, president of the United Mine Workers, maintained that the strike was a just one.

Near Aguilar, the Empire mine was besieged, the tipple burned, the mouth of the slope caved in by dynamite explosions. Governor Ammons reported an attack on Delagua and Hastings by miners, and Trinidad's mayor and Chamber of Commerce appealed to President Wilson for aid. An attack on the Berwind mine was expected momentarily.

Two hundred militia and company guards along the tracks at Ludlow were cut off from the rest of the district, according to the *Times,* by "armed bands of strikers whose ranks are swelled constantly by men who swarm over the hills from all directions." Three mine guards were reported dead at Aguilar and two mine shafts were in ashes. The press reported that "the hills in every direction seem suddenly to be alive with men."

At Colorado Springs, three hundred union miners quit work to go to the Trinidad district, carrying revolvers, rifles, and shotguns.

The union charged that the National Guard was exploding dynamite in the holes under the tents at Ludlow, to destroy evidence of further loss of life. As for Congress, a headline read, "SENATE AND HOUSE MEMBERS EXPRESS VIEWS BUT TAKE NO ACTION."

A dispatch from Pueblo reported the first legal action. A federal grand jury had returned indictments against eight striking miners on charges of attacking the company post office at Higgins, Colorado.

As a troop train was readied to leave Denver to carry soldiers to the strike zone, the eighty-two men of Company C mutinied and refused to go to the district. According to the *New York Times,* "The men declared they would not engage in the shooting of women and children. They hissed the 350 men who did start and shouted imprecations at them."

A million dollars in damage had reportedly been done in the first two days of the fighting, and the newspapers followed the story closely. A Denver reporter wrote, "Interest today centered in the progress of the troop train sent from Denver to the Ludlow district. One thousand armed strikers met last night to halt the progress of the train."

On April 27, 1914, headlines in the *Times* read, "WILSON TO SEND FEDERAL TROOPS TO COLORADO. AMMONS CALLED TRAITOR. GREAT MASS MEETING OF DENVER CITIZENS DENOUNCE HIM AND LIEUTENANT GOVERNOR FITZGERALD. ASSAIL ROCKEFELLER JR. MEN AND WOMEN WEEP AS BLANCHE BATES' HUSBAND READS RESOLUTION. STRIKERS CAPTURE CHANDLER AFTER TWO DAY BATTLE." The press reported that there was great difficulty getting federal troops because all nearby military posts had been stripped to provide a patrol along the Mexican border.

At the Denver meeting, a crowd of five thousand men and women stood in the pouring rain on the lawn in front of the capital. George Creel, former police commissioner of Denver, read the resolution, asking that Major Hamrock, Lieutenant Linderfelt, and other National Guard officers be tried for murder, and that the state seize the mines and operate them. They branded the governor and lieutenant governor of Colorado as "traitors to the people and accessories to the murder of babies at Ludlow."

While that meeting was in progress, the Denver Cigar Makers Union voted to send five hundred armed men to Ludlow and Trinidad in the morning. The women of the Denver United Garment Workers Union announced that four hundred of their members had volunteered as nurses to aid the Colorado strikers.

Governor Ammons acted. He appointed a special board of officers, consisting of Major Edward J. Boughton and two infantry captains, to report on the massacre. The Boughton Report concluded that the National Guard was friendly to the strikers, except for Company B, headed by Linderfelt. The report blamed Linderfelt for being "tactless." Upon the withdrawal of the National Guard troops from the field, one unit had to remain behind, it stated, and Company B had been selected "because, although hated by the strikers, it was feared and respected by them."

"The tent colony population is almost wholly foreign and without conception of our government," said the report. "A large percentage are unassimilable aliens to whom liberty means license. . . . Rabid agitators had assured these people that when the soldiers left they were at liberty to take for their own, and by force of arms, the coal mines of their former employers. . . . They prepared for battle."

The Boughton Report found the coal operators only remotely responsible, for having "established in an American industrial community a numerous class of ignorant, lawless, and savage South-European peasants." But the immediate cause of the violence was seen as the action of Greek strikers in attacking the militia: "The Greeks were the leaders. . . . The conflict was deliberately planned by some of the strikers."

The report recommended that a general court martial should try all officers and men who had mistreated, killed, burned, or looted; that a permanent constabulary should be set up to curb "ferocious foreigners"; that all "instigators" should be apprehended and punished; and that the reestablishment of the Ludlow tent colony be forbidden.

The left wing of the American labor movement made its contrasting sentiments very clear. Eugene Debs wrote in the *International Socialist Review*, "Like the shot at Lexington on April 20 in another year, the shots fired at Ludlow were heard around the world. . . . It is more historic than Lexington and . . . will prove, as we believe, the signal for the American industrial revolution." Another article by Debs called for a Gunmen Defense Fund, with "the latest high power rifles, the same ones used by the corporation gunmen, and 500 rounds of cartridges. In addition to this, every district should purchase and equip and man enough Gatling and machine guns to match the equipment of Rockefeller's private army of assassins. This suggestion is made advisedly, and I hold myself responsible for every word of it." Mother Jones told a House of Representatives committee, "The laboring man is tired of working to build up millions so that millionaires' wives may wear diamonds."

With the National Guard in Colorado unable to control the mounting waves of violence, damages mounting to many millions of dollars, and over twenty killed since the massacre, Governor Ammons requested that President Wilson send in federal troops.

According to Upton Sinclair (who sometimes exaggerated), on the day the federal troops were sent, the miners had dynamite under all the railroad tracks into Trinidad, ready to blow them up, two million rounds of ammunition at a piano warehouse, and fifteen hundred men in a neighboring state, armed and pledged to march over the mountains.

On April 29 President Wilson proclaimed, "Whereas it is provided by the Constitution of the United States (that the U.S. shall protect states, upon application against domestic violence) . . . now, therefore, I warn all persons . . . to disperse and retire peaceably to their respective abodes on or before the 30th day of April, instant."

Secretary of War Garrison asked all parties to surrender their arms. The commander of the federal troops prohibited the import of strikebreakers from other states, prohibited picketing, and protected scabs.

Finally, the fighting ended.

President Wilson appointed a committee to mediate peace, which then drew up a series of proposals. The union accepted. The operators refused. The committee ended its work.

The House Mines and Mining subcommittee assembled to investigate the strike called John D. Rockefeller to testify shortly afterward. Rockefeller was now the object of both sharp attack and vigorous defense. He told the committee he had not visited Colorado for ten years or attended Colorado Fuel & Iron directors' meetings during that period. He said he had not the "slightest idea" of wages or conditions in the mines.

However, according to the report of the Commission on Industrial Relations, Rockefeller had "followed, step by step, the struggle of his executive officials to retain arbitrary power, and to prevent the installation of machinery for collective bargaining, by which abuses might automatically be corrected, and he supported and encouraged this struggle in every letter he wrote to his agents." (The Commission on Industrial Relations had been set up in 1912 by the Senate at President Wilson's request to find a solution for increasing capital-labor conflict. It was headed by a former labor attorney named Frank Walsh, and later held hearings on the Colorado coal strike.)

Rockefeller told the House committee that the strike had cost Colorado Fuel & Iron over a million dollars but that "we stand ready to lose every cent to defend the workers' right to work." A member of the committee asked, "You'll do that, even if you lose all your money, and have all your employees killed?" Rockefeller answered, "It's a great principle. It's a national issue."

Another version of this statement, reported by John Reed, who came up from his travels with the revolutionary Pancho Villa's forces in Mexico to cover the story of the massacre and wrote several eloquent articles for the *Metropolitan Magazine,* Rockefeller said, "We would rather that the unfortunate conditions continue, and that we should lose all the millions invested, than that the American workmen should be deprived of their right, under the Constitution, to work for whom they please. That is the great principle at stake."

But Rockefeller was clearly disturbed by the bad name he was getting throughout the country. Picketers, including the novelist Upton Sinclair, had marched outside his New York offices at 26 Broadway, near the churches where Rockefeller worshipped, and around Rockefeller's Tarrytown estate.

Deciding he needed to change the public perception of him as being responsible for the brutal murders in Colorado, he hired Ivy Lee, who had been recommended to him as "the father of public relations in the United States." Lee, who had worked for the Pennsylvania Railroad to make the high rates it was charging palatable to the public, described his work as "the art of getting believed in."

Rockefeller hired Lee for $1,000 a month, and Lee put out a series of tracts labeled "Facts Concerning the Struggle in Colorado for Industrial Freedom," but his "facts" were all designed to portray the miners in the most ugly light, and included questioning the personal morals of Mother Jones. Radical publications referred to Lee as "Poison Ivy."

Rockefeller considered himself an enlightened man, devoted to Christian principles. In 1913 he had founded the Bureau of Social Hygiene, dedicated to study and cure the evil of prostitution. He had read a good deal, even Karl Marx's *Capital.* "And yet," writes Zeese Papanikolas, biographer of Lou Tikas, "what reading he did, his study, only had the effect of broadening the prejudices he had begun with, after all."

In the seven months after the Ludlow Massacre, the air was filled with talk of negotiations, peace offers, mediation plans. Rockefeller got together with Mackenzie King of Canada, a politician experienced in labor disputes, and later to become prime minister of Canada. What emerged was the Rockefeller Industrial Representation Plan, a substitute for unionism whereby workers would select representatives to discuss problems with management—in effect, a company union.

The talks continued, the hearings went on. Testimony totaling 5,500 pages was heard by the Industrial Relations Commission and the House Mines and Mining subcommittee while federal troops patrolled the strike area.

Based on the report of the investigating committee set up under Major Boughton by order of Governor Ammons, a military court held a series of court-martials of militiamen accused of crimes. They hurried through the trial of ten enlisted men, acquitting them all, then came to Lieutenant Karl Linderfelt. Linderfelt admitted clubbing Lou Tikas with a rifle, admitted this was unsoldierly, but said that "any man who curses me has got the same thing coming." There was testimony that the rifle stock that broke over Tikas' head had been weak. The court martial found Linderfelt guilty of assaulting Tikas with a Springfield rifle, "but attaches no criminality thereto. And the court does therefore acquit him."

With the guardsmen exonerated, the authorities could now deal with the strikers. In May of 1914, John R. Lawson, the leader of the strike, was tried for murder. Judge Granby Hillyer, before whom he was tried, was appointed by the governor after serving as attorney for Colorado Fuel & Iron and assisting in the preparation of other cases against the strikers. The panel from which the jury was chosen was selected by the sheriff of Las Animas County. Lawson was accused of murdering John Nimmo, one of the army of deputies paid by the mining companies and appointed by the sheriff. No effort was made to prove that Lawson fired the fatal shot; he was to be held responsible because he led the strike and was at the Ludlow tent colony on the day of the battle. Sheriff Jefferson Farr of Huerfano County testified that for all he knew, the deputies might have been the murderers. Lawson was convicted.

The Colorado Coal Strike, 1913–14

The Commission on Industrial Relations, consistently friendly to the miners, called his conviction "anarchism for profits and revenge, [which] menaces the security and integrity of American institutions as they seldom have been menaced before." Lawson's conviction was eventually overturned.

On December 10, 1914, a special United Mine Workers convention at Denver called off the strike. The union had not won recognition. Sixty-six men, women, and children had been killed. Not one militiaman or mine guard had been convicted of a crime. The following month, Mother Jones told a crowd in Cooper Union that the union had "had only the Constitution. The other side had the bayonets. In the end, bayonets always win."

The final report of the subcommittee of the House Mines and Mining Committee was printed in 1915. The committee had been asked to determine whether peonage existed in the coalfields; whether postal facilities had been violated; whether immigration laws had been broken; whether citizens had been arrested, tried, or convicted in violation of the Constitution or the laws of the United States; whether interstate commerce had been interfered with. The conclusion of the committee was that, "if any federal law can be enacted to stop such industrial disturbances, Congress should act." No specific law was suggested. The separate views of several of the subcommittee members were added. Congressman James F. Byrnes, of South Carolina, later to be secretary of state and adviser to President Harry Truman in the dropping of the bomb on Hiroshima, declared that no federal laws had been violated and therefore nothing could be done.

Of the Rockefeller–Mackenzie King plan, Samuel Yellen, who chronicled the strike in his book *American Labor Struggles* (1936), wrote, "This plan . . . was the only fruit won by the coal miners of southern Colorado after their long and bloody struggle." This was a superficial estimate. The strike and the Ludlow Massacre had affected the consciousness of millions of Americans in a way that could not be easily measured.

Little by little, news dispatches about the Colorado strike and its aftermath grew less numerous, until they disappeared altogether. After World War I, a brief strike at the Colorado Fuel & Iron mines was won by the I.W.W., but the union petered away. In 1928, violence flared again in another strike. The United Mine Workers came back, this time for good.

In the thirties, came the rise of the C.I.O. (Congress of Industrial Organizations) and a new wave of militant trade unionism.

Woody Guthrie was moved to write a song, which he entitled "The Ludlow Massacre." Here are two of its eleven stanzas:

> You struck a match and the blaze it started.
> You pulled the triggers of your gatling guns.
> I made a run for the children but the fire wall stopped me.
> Thirteen children died from your guns. . . .

> We took some cement and walled that cave up
> Where you killed those thirteen children inside.
> I said, "God bless the Mine Workers' Union,"
> And then I hung my head and cried.

Today, on an isolated patch of desert in southern Colorado, in the shadow of the black hills, stands a monument erected by the United Mine Workers on the spot where the death pit of the Ludlow Massacre existed. The monument lists the names of the individuals found in the pit and declares its dedication "to those who gave their lives for freedom at Ludlow."

Cedelina Costa	Eulala Valdez
Lucy Costa	Rudolph Valdez
Carlo Costa	Frank Petrucci
Onafrio Costa	Joe Petrucci
Parria Valdez	Lucy Petrucci
Elvira Valdez	Cloriva Pedragon
Mary Valdez	

The Colorado Coal Strike, 1913–14

The strike in Colorado, like so many struggles of people through the ages, has often been seen as a defeat for the workers. Certainly it was, at the time. But for those who came to know of the event—mostly outside the classroom—in the decades since the Ludlow Massacre, the story has been educational and inspiring.

We learn something about the symbiotic relationship between giant corporations and government. We learn about the selective control of violence, where the authorities deal one way with the violence of workers and another way with the violence of police and militia. We learn about the role of the mainstream press. At the same time, we are inspired by those ordinary men and women who persist, with extraordinary courage, in their resistance to overwhelming power. It is a story that continues in our time.

DANA FRANK

~ ~ ~ ~ ~

GIRL STRIKERS OCCUPY CHAIN STORE, WIN BIG:
The Detroit Woolworth's Strike of 1937

ON THE SURFACE it seemed like the most ordinary of Saturdays at the most ordinary of American institutions. It was February 27, 1937, at Woolworth's Five and Dime store, the big four-story red brick one in downtown Detroit, at the corner of Grand River and Woodward Avenue. Like all Woolworth's stores, this one was painted with red and green trim, with the chain's name out front in big gold letters. Throughout that morning cabs and buses, Chryslers and Plymouths slid back and forth along the avenue. Shoppers rustled by or paused for a brief chat with friends.

Inside, Woolworth's opened up like a palace, with fluted columns, embossed tin ceiling tiles, hanging bulbous art nouveau lamps, and, best of all, a vast array of small, low-priced goods: hair combs, knitting needles, lampshades, safety pins, pie plates, face creams, and crisp new shoelaces folded into little packets with paper bands around their middles specifying their length. Most wonderfully, Woolworth's was a palace built for working-class people. The big fluted columns were made of concrete, not marble, then painted shiny bright colors. Tidily printed signs poked up from displays throughout the store to reassure customers that almost all the goods splayed out in flat, tray-like counters at waist level cost only

[59]

five or ten cents, just as the store's name promised. Bins of tilted glass along one side held back masses of eminently affordable jelly beans, peanut clusters, and old-fashioned mystery candies with names of obscure origin like "bridge mix" or "nonpareils" (the little chocolate mounds with white sprinkles embedded in their tops that survive today in the equally obscure realm of movie theater candy).

Unlike its Costco and Price Club heirs, Woolworth's promised not a cavernous warehouse of cardboard boxes in monster sizes, but a maze of small nooks and crannies, up and down stairs, waiting to be discovered. Shoppers in downtown Detroit that Saturday could weave upward to the second floor on wide wooden stairs with a brass railing down their middle, pause on the landing at a glass display full of woven pastel Easter baskets and Peter Rabbits (it was three weeks before Easter) and pass upward to a "complete line of knitting and crotcheting" with "free instruction," and to the delights of the notions and dry goods departments. The more intrepid could follow arrows luring them down into the basement sales level, complete with canaries. There, shoppers who were white could indulge in a banana split at the lunch counter.

The hundred and fifty or so young women working at Woolworth's on this particular morning seemed like the most ordinary of young working-class ladies. Sandwiched behind the displays, gracefully sidestepping piles of boxes kept out of the customers' sight, the clerks flashed smiles, made change, or cheerfully introduced the latest lipstick. The ones who worked in the candy department and at the lunch counter wore little white short-sleeved uniforms with colored cuffs and collars and matching plastic buttons. The salesclerks, by contrast, were wearing surprisingly dressy outfits in somber colors—long, sleek, fitted skirts and knitted tops with short jackets or wide lace collars. Most wore heels, though not the waitresses, who had on the 1930s version of sensible shoes. Almost every single one of the women had the exact same hairdo: cut just a bit below her chin, parted on the side, and curving down in carefully constructed waves around her face.

Girl Strikers Occupy Chain Store, Win Big

Suddenly, at exactly 11:00 A.M., at the height of the Saturday shopping rush, Floyd Loew, an organizer for the Waiters' and Waitresses' Union of Detroit, strode to the very center of the store's first floor. Without warning he blew a screeching whistle as loud as he could and yelled, "STRIKE! STRIKE!" (by some reports, "STRIKE, girls, STRIKE!").

Voices shouted out and cheers rose from different parts of the store. First the women in the white uniforms at the food counter stopped working. Then they moved quickly through the whole store, and soon almost all the women workers on all three sales floors had stepped back from their counters or rushed out from the kitchen, folded their arms, and stopped working, clearly in accordance with a tightly coordinated plan.

"Behind the counters, the girls appeared ready for the call," reported the *Detroit News*. "The jangle of cash registers stopped, and bewildered customers found themselves holding out nickels and dimes in vain." A small number of women, maybe ten or fifteen, kept working for a while, and seem to have slipped quietly out of the store in the chaos that followed. One news report alleged that Floyd Loew, the union organizer, yelled out, "Sock any of those girls who don't stop working." But "there was no trouble," said the *Detroit Times*. "Not a girl tried to wait on a customer."

A floor supervisor rushed off to find the store's manager, William F. Mayer. Within minutes, Mayer and all the women, plus assorted stock boys, department heads, and managers, along with Loew and other organizers from the waiters' and waitresses' union, had crammed into a conference room on the third floor. The strikers presented Mayer with an explicit set of demands: they would refuse to work and would occupy the store night and day until Woolworth's granted them union recognition, a ten-cent an hour raise (they were making around twenty-five cents an hour), an eight-hour workday, time and a half for overtime after forty-eight hours a week, fifty-cent lunches for the soda fountain workers, free uniforms and free laundering of them, seniority rights, hiring of new workers only through the union offices, and no discrimination against the strikers after they returned to work.

Mayer hurriedly tried to "sweettalk" the women into returning to work. He promised he'd do everything he could to address their concerns on Monday—if only they'd all, please, please, go back to work.

"Alright girls, give him your answer," shouted Loew. "NO!" they roared. And there was no turning back.

A hundred and eight ordinary young women had done a huge, astonishing thing: they were not only on strike, right in the depths of the Great Depression, but they were occupying the property of one of the largest transnational companies in the United States and refusing to leave until they won. It was a classic sit-down strike, but for the first time the strikers were all women working in a variety store, not men in a factory. Within hours the eyes of the nation would be riveted on these young women and their strike. They had, after all, taken on one of the biggest corporate and consumer icons of the century, with two thousand stores in five countries—it was like striking Wal-Mart, the Gap, and McDonald's all at the same time.

These young women believed that they just might win because they were living in an extraordinary moment in history, in the exact geographic epicenter of the labor uprisings of the Great Depression. At that very moment union activists were breaking out of the straightjacket of the American Federation of Labor (AFL) to give birth to the militant Congress of Industrial Organizations (CIO). In a mass uprising of almost four million working people in the late 1930s and early 1940s, young people were on the move; the Left was thriving; new tactics of canny strategy and direct action, especially the sit-down strike, were suddenly deployed with both daring and shocking success. It wasn't exactly a revolution, but something huge was happening in early 1937.

And from February 27 to March 5, the Woolworth strikers were at center stage. Newsreel teams, radio personalities, and reporters from the *New York Times, Chicago Tribune,* and *Life* magazine rushed to Detroit to cover the story. As the press well knew, the salesclerks and waitresses at Woolworth's had set something huge in motion that would have ripple effects in the labor movement, in popular culture, and in the lives of everyone involved for decades to come. No question, these strikers had taken on Goliath. It was both thrilling and terrifying—and the consequences were utterly uncertain.

CHAIN STORE MENACE GROWING

Today if we think of Woolworth's, we either recall the battles to desegregate its lunchrooms in the early 1960s or evoke a romantic image of small-town life gone by, paved under by the consolidating forces of modern consumer capitalism. But in the 1930s Woolworth's was itself the modernizer, bulldozing down an earlier generation of small merchants and offering shoppers not the old-fashioned but the new and stylish. In the process it spat out enormous profits for its owners. By the mid-1930s, though, the public was beginning to get clear about where those profits came from—and at what price.

Frank W. Woolworth, the firm's president until his death in 1919, opened his first store in Lancaster, Pennsylvania, in 1879. Woolworth figured out that he could draw in masses of working-class shoppers and make hefty profits by offering an entire store full of ultra-cheap goods, none of them priced at more than five or ten cents, hence the new name "five and dime." Within a few years Woolworth had opened seven stores in upstate New York and Pennsylvania; by 1905 he had a hundred and twenty stores all over the country; by 1937 he had over two thousand. Woolworth's immediately leapt across national borders. Between 1897 and 1900 alone the company opened fifty-nine stores in Canada. By 1913, Frank Woolworth had come of age as a famous magnate, big enough to erect his own monument, the Woolworth Building, a sixty-story neo-gothic tower at the corner of Broadway and Park Place in New York City.

In part, Frank Woolworth's secret was all those inexpensive, useful objects—the safety pins, shoelaces, and pie plates. But he had also figured out that people would buy all sorts of other "novelty goods," another now old-fashioned concept that was innovative in its time. He sold millions of holiday decorations, for example, like the Easter bunnies on display in Detroit at the end of February in 1937, or glass ornaments for Christmas trees and funny green hats for St. Patrick's Day. His stores also catered to fads. Whatever hair clip happened to be in fashion that month, he stocked by the millions. And Woolworth also figured out there was money to be made off children, especially by selling candy; in 1917 alone the chain sold ninety million pounds. Woolworth's also established its famous segregated lunch counters, selling banana splits for pennies. Overall, even if the profit was miniscule on each nonpareil or chocolate sundae, the volume of total sales added up quickly. In 1935 Woolworth's produced a profit of $31,247,000.

Frank Woolworth also pioneered in the structural elements that could make economies of scale lucrative. He introduced a centralized, pooled ordering system, regional warehouses, and regular buying forays to Europe. In the process his company developed enormous power over its suppliers, as it began to skip past the wholesalers to buy directly from manufacturers—just as Wal-Mart and its rivals do today. "The syndicate would absorb a factory's entire output under the terms of year-long contracts," notes James Brough in his study of the Woolworth family. "Frank dictated the terms to those manufacturers; the price of their security was subservience." With large markets assured, the suppliers could save by avoiding credit costs and buying raw materials in bulk. But Mr. Woolworth called the shots on price, quality, shipment dates, and future contracts.

Girl Strikers Occupy Chain Store, Win Big

Woolworth's goods were also cheap because Frank and his minions became adept at sniffing out the products of sweated labor. In one account of a buying trip, Woolworth told of visiting a poor mountain village in Germany where impoverished women and children labored night and day, heads bent, making little wax dolls and Christmas tree ornaments. Ah, Mr. Woolworth lamented, they were so oppressed. He immediately placed a big order.

At the time of the Detroit strike, the Woolworth Corporation was a powerful presence all over North America and across the Atlantic. That year Woolworth's owned 2010 stores in the United States, Canada, and Cuba, plus 737 stores in Britain and 82 in Germany.

But just as the company grew and grew, a broad social movement mushroomed with equal energy in the late 1920s and 1930s, dedicated to stopping the spread of chain stores like Woolworth's. By 1928, organizations dedicated to eradicating what they called the chain store evil were thriving in over four hundred communities across the United States. Almost entirely lost to historical memory, the movement expanded throughout the early and mid-1930s and reached its peak at almost the exact same moment as the Detroit strike in 1937.

Critics pointed out that stores like Woolworth's had been marching across the national landscape at an ever-increasing pace since the 1920s. The chains' share of total retail sales grew from 4 percent in 1919 to 20 percent in 1929 and was still expanding. The A&P grocery chain alone owned 15,000 stores by 1929; chain groceries altogether accounted for over 39 percent of all grocery sales in the country that year. Drugstores, cigar stores, shoe stores—in all these fields, chains were rapidly pushing aside locally owned businesses and independent merchants. In the variety store market Woolworth's dominated, well ahead of its closest rival, S. S. Kresge, with 1,881 stores in 1930 to Kresge's 678.

Small merchants in particular charged that the chains were "a menace to the community." As a letter circulated in Indiana put it, "The chain stores are undermining the foundation of our entire local happiness and prosperity. They have destroyed our home markets and merchants, paying a minimum to our local enterprises and charity, sapping the life-blood of prosperous communities"—sort of like corporate vampires. Small merchants couldn't compete with the chains' vast economies of scale, the critics charged, and as smaller stores went under, jobs for owners and their trainees were evaporating, leaving "a nation of clerks." Wholesalers were also being squeezed out by the growing intimacy between chain stores and suppliers, and they too jumped into the fray. By the mid-1930s the movement against chain stores had become extremely popular. A poll in August of 1936 found that 69 percent of Americans believed the chains were dangerous and should be suppressed.

In response, between 1934 and 1941 state legislators introduced five hundred bills containing measures designed to curb the chains. Most of the proposed laws imposed a hefty graduated tax that grew steeper as the number of stores in the chain grew, and most were quickly ruled unconstitutional, but thirty-two survived. In 1928, as criticism mounted, Congress ordered the Federal Trade Commission to investigate the chains. Its report, issued in 1935, came out pro-chain. But meanwhile the mere fact that the federal government was investigating the chains confirmed popular concerns, further legitimating the anti-chain movement. The movement's greatest triumph was the Robinson-Patman Act of 1936, an amendment to the Clayton Antitrust Act of 1914. Robinson-Patman addressed the supply end, making it illegal for manufacturers to offer differential discounts to retail buyers based on the quantity of their orders, if the effect would be "to lessen competition or tend to create a monopoly."

By the mid-1930s the chains felt deeply threatened by all this agitation—the proposed taxes alone would have cost them millions. Woolworth's, as one of the largest and most visible of these retail empires, would have felt especially vulnerable. Very quickly the chains spent thousands on advertisements, lobbyists, and even a clever little *Debate Manual on the Chain Store Question* that purported to offer tips for arguing both sides but always circled back around to the dangers of regulation. By 1937, they had pushed back their critics and stopped the anti-chain movement's advance. Woolworth's public relations problem #1 had been successfully contained for the time being, but its ghost would remain, hovering behind the strike to come.

BABS SPENDS MILLIONS ON NEW HUBBY IN ORGY OF SPENDING

The company's executives, though, could never contain their public relations problem #2, Woolworth heiress Barbara Hutton. Hutton proved an eternal public relations migraine because she unmasked one of the company's dirty secrets: how much money was being made and how offensively it was being spent. And when the Detroit sit-down blasted across the nation's headlines in 1937, Barbara Hutton loomed larger than ever in the public imagination.

Barbara was Frank Woolworth's granddaughter, born in 1912. Her mother, Edna Woolworth, had married eternal playboy Franklyn Hutton, brother to the famous broker E. F. Hutton. When Barbara, their only child, was four, Edna killed herself with poison. Barbara spent the next two years under the care of governesses, wandering about in her grandfather's mansion in New York. Then, in 1919, her grandfather passed on to wherever chain store magnates go, soon to be joined by his wife Jennie, and in 1924 the Woolworth fortune passed to their two surviving daughters plus little Barbara, in three equal shares.

That left Barbara "the richest girl in the world," as the press and its readers dubbed her, riveted by the prospect of her vast future wealth. For a time her father took an interest in her, but soon she was old enough to be packed off to boarding school in the East.

"Babs" became a fixture in the media throughout the 1920s, the proverbial pampered, unhappy, ultra-rich semi-orphan for whom the phrase "poor little rich girl" was originally coined.

Then the Depression hit, and Barbara came of age. Her self-indulgent persona blossomed, and everyone knew about it from daily press reports. She was infatuated with spending money—on jewels, on designer clothes, on cars, and especially on men. Out of some vast romantic fantasy and who knows what deep-seated insecurities she had developed during her famously unhappy childhood, Hutton was fixated on marrying European royalty. In 1933, five months before she turned twenty-one and could assume full control over her estate, she married Count Alexis Mdivani (with a nicely pretentious silent *M*), a Russian emigré gold digger with a dubious claim to a Georgian title. The press went wild. At the celebrity wedding of the decade Barbara wore a diamond tiara, bracelet, and pearls, altogether worth a million dollars (about twelve million in 2000 dollars). She bought eighty outfits for her honeymoon, seventy trunks for the servants to cart them around in, and for her wedding night a nightgown that had been embroidered by two dozen cloistered nuns.

Later that year Barbara came into full possession of her fortune, an estimated $50 million (about $600 million in 2000 dollars). As the press obsessively recounted her wealth over the next three years, "Babs" kept up the show in escalating performances of spending, traveling all over the world and throwing money around with proverbial reckless abandon. By 1937 she had dumped her first prince and married another, Count Kurt Haugwitz-Reventlow, this one a minor member of the vestigial Danish landed nobility. That year—the year of the Detroit strike—she bought jewelry worth $2 million, a Packard, a yellow convertible, two Rolls-Royces, a 157-foot yacht, and a mansion-estate in London. The latter cost about $4.5 million and featured two ten-car garages, a boathouse, stables, tennis courts, two pools (one indoor, one outdoor), and, best of all, a bathroom made of $10,000 worth of marble, with sink and bathtub handles of gold, shelves of crystal, and heated towel racks. She employed thirty-one servants to keep it all neat and tidy.

All this wealth, self-indulgence, and obliviousness would be obscene in the best of times, but seven years into the Great Depression it was beyond appalling to most Americans. The Poor Little Rich Girl became the Most Hated Girl in America. "There has always been something fantastic and a little useless and stupid about Barbara Hutton," wrote columnist Adela Rogers St. John in 1937. Wherever Barbara went in the United States, cab drivers snubbed her and doormen slammed doors in her face. And wherever she went she carried the "Woolworth heiress" tag along with her. (Although she had sold a large hunk of her domestic Woolworth stock in 1930, she still owned part of the British subsidiary, and even if invested elsewhere, the money had all come from grandpa Woolworth.) Much to the chagrin of the Woolworth executives of her day, Barbara Hutton Mdivani Haugwitz-Reventlow's crime was not so much that she was rich, but that—unlike her aunts, for example, who were every bit as wealthy—she failed to follow all the unspoken rules of discretion by which the super-rich mask their wealth, enjoy it behind closed doors, and represent themselves to the public as tasteful and benevolent.

TIRED FEET, SAY FIVE AND DIME CLERKS

If Barbara Hutton focused public attention on Woolworth profits by showing exactly where they went, she also highlighted where they came from, because in the eyes of the press her antithesis was the poor, exploited young woman who labored as a Woolworth's clerk. In 1933 Bing Crosby released the hit song that would entwine the two in the public imagination for decades: "I Found a Million-Dollar Baby in a Five-and-Ten-Cent Store."

Woolworth's goods were so very cheap in part because the people that sold them were paid the lowest possible wages. Frank

Woolworth put his formula bluntly: "We must have cheap help or we cannot sell cheap goods." More precisely, he couldn't make huge profits and keep expanding if he couldn't obtain inexpensive labor to keep his profit margin up.

To keep its labor costs in the basement, Woolworth's deliberately deskilled its sales operation—that is, it made its clerks' jobs as simple as possible. "The Woolworth chain takes the position that the salesgirls are primarily wrapping and change-making machines and they make little effort to pick for sales ability," observed one industry analyst in 1928. Woolworth's pioneered in placing its goods out on display, easily accessible to the customer, who no longer had to ask a clerk to fetch down a particularly enticing lampshade from an upper shelf behind a counter. The company bet correctly that if enough appealing objects were available at cheap enough prices, the goods would sell themselves and Woolworth's would save big bucks on labor. "When a clerk gets so good she can get better wages elsewhere let her go," Frank Woolworth wrote as early as 1892, "for it does not require skilled and expensive salesladies to sell our goods."

Woolworth's formula is the same one used by McDonald's, Circuit City, and other big chains today. If the job is sufficiently deskilled, a huge potential labor pool opens up, and if turnover rates are high, so much the better—managers can then pick and choose the pliant, the eager, and the charming. By the 1930s, Woolworth's had developed labor policies that deliberately created a revolving door of employment. Store managers were rotated from store to store and encouraged to weed out employees regularly at each new site. And since the mid-nineteenth century employers had used another, accompanying trick: after deskilling the job, hire women—especially young women—who had very few choices on the labor market, who might see themselves working for pay only temporarily, and who, in theory, were less likely to unionize.

In 1937, Woolworth's employed about sixty-two thousand people in the United States, but never hired any African Americans. Or at least its managers didn't think they did. Throughout the mid-twentieth century, women of partial African descent passed as white, often by posing as Italian or Spanish, to obtain relatively good jobs as clerks in variety and department stores. However much these jobs were dead-end, poorly paid, and exhausting, they were a vast improvement over almost anything else available to Black women, leading hundreds of women who passed as white to endure the pain of hearing coworkers' racist remarks day after day in order to support their families.

Almost all the women who worked at Woolworth's in 1937 were very young. According to a national survey of Woolworth workers in 1930, about half the store's employees were sixteen, seventeen, or eighteen years old, a quarter were between nineteen and twenty-four, and only around 17 percent were twenty-five or older. Judging by photos of the Detroit strike, though, a very few of the Detroit workers were in their thirties or forties. Some, at the other end, were fourteen or fifteen. Former Detroit Woolworth's employee Ceil McDougle, for example, remembers working at the chain in 1935 when she was only fifteen.

The women were overwhelmingly native born, and most were of western or northern European descent, like McDougle, whose parents were English and Scottish. Some of the clerks and waitresses at Woolworth's were married, but most were single women who lived with their parents, turned their paychecks dutifully over to their elders, and got a few dollars slipped back now and again for a new dress or a pair of shoes.

Working at Woolworth's could be grueling. Although some worked only part-time or seasonally—Ceil McDougle worked only at Christmas, Easter, and other holidays—most worked around fifty hours every week, six days a week, and over a third regularly put in more than fifty-four hours. That meant nine hours a day, standing up. And that, in turn, meant very painful feet. "I don't know how the other girls stand it," sympathized a New York Woolworth's worker who had shelled out eight dollars for special shoes.

"They get flat feet and fallen arches and little surface varicose veins." State labor laws might dictate a stool for every woman to rest on, but clerks at Woolworth's in New York laughed at the idea of getting to sit. "All the old girls know you can't sit down, no matter how slow it is and how tired you are." When business lagged, the salesclerks had to look busy or they'd be confronted by floor managers or fake shoppers lurking about to spy on them. If a waitress lacked customers, she was expected to scrub the shelves or those big concrete columns—that was why the paint looked so shiny and bright all the time.

Managers could be capricious or mean. As Ceil McDougle put it politely, with an understated sigh, "Well, they didn't have your interests at heart." Or, as a New York Woolworth's employee put it in 1939, "The manager's very grouchy. . . . If he says black is red, then black is red." Store managers tended to create a hierarchy of women's employment correlated with perceived beauty. The loveliest often got the better jobs as salesclerks, lunch counter waitresses were one notch down, and kitchen helpers ranked lowest on the ladder of perceived attractiveness and concomitant income and workload. The clerks got $14.50, the waitresses $13.50 a week (plus the latter had to pay for their uniforms and to have them laundered, although they would have received some additional income from tips). Lower-level managers, all male, also had their pets—workers who they thought were cute, from whom they might obtain a sexual favor, or who pleased them with a seemingly subservient manner.

All in all, by 1937 Woolworth's had built a powerful engine of wealth and poverty, a private empire that spread to Cuba and Germany, into small-town life and into the daily lives of tens of thousands of young women. But by the late 1930s the workings of that engine were also becoming increasingly visible to the American public. Woolworth's might be a great place to buy pie plates or Fourth of July bunting, but Barbara Hutton's exploits were sickening, the chains were being cast as an evil menace, and the woman behind the counter had a glazed, exhausted look in her eye—people saw it. Soon enough, all those public perceptions would turn out to be powerful weapons in the hands of the strikers.

AUTOWORKERS IN BIG VICTORY OVER GENERAL MOTORS; STAY-INS SPREADING

Woolworth's was a formidable opponent, but the women who clerked at the Detroit Woolworth's weren't stupid in taking on such an immense adversary. This was the 1930s, after all, and they were sniffing the activist wind. In the middle of the Great Depression, just when working people should have been feeling most vulnerable, most powerless, most at the mercy of corporations, the tide of labor activism rushed in and millions of ordinary working people suddenly believed in their own power and unleashed it.

The Great Depression had hit hard and stayed hard. By 1933 one-third of the country's workforce was unemployed and another third was underemployed, working part-time or in marginal jobs. Production plummeted by two-thirds; bankruptcies rippled through cities, schools, banks, and small businesses, tearing apart families. President Franklin Delano Roosevelt, inaugurated in 1933, promised to close the economic abyss, but the first elements of his New Deal, while they provided direct aid for the poor, did not yet address structural changes in the economy.

The mere hint of federal support for the labor movement in the National Industrial Recovery Act of 1933, however, prompted a wave of strikes and organizing drives in 1933 and 1934. Cotton pickers in California, textile workers in the South, garment workers in New York, waterfront workers in San Francisco, teamsters in Minneapolis—all organized by the hundreds of thousands and launched mass strikes, proving that working people were eager to join unions and anything but passive in the face of economic devastation.

But they had one big problem on their hands: the American

Federation of Labor (AFL). After a decade of governmental repression following World War I, most of the labor unions that had remained in the early 1930s AFL were narrow, largely interested in skilled workers only, and spectacularly suspicious and conservative in their attitude toward organizing new workers, especially women or people of color, whom they mostly excluded. Most AFL unions were obsessed with petty jurisdictional disputes over which union had the right to represent which exact workers, depending on narrow skill categories. (The federation's opponents called it the American Separation of Labor.)

Then, in 1935, Congress passed the National Labor Relations Act, also known as the Wagner Act, to deliberately encourage unionization and collective bargaining through a complex system of supervised elections, negotiations, and, above all, protection of the right to organize. The moment had come for labor to rise up. But unless something could be done to crack open the AFL, nothing would move, and progressive activists knew it.

Enter the CIO. In late 1935, leaders of several of the more militant unions in the AFL formed a new coalition, the Committee for Industrial Organization, the original CIO. They quickly drew up plans for a mass organizing drive that would embrace all workers in broad, industry-by-industry unions, and started to pool their funds. Deeply threatened by these militants and their energetic plans, the AFL leadership suspended all of the CIO's unions in late summer of 1936. Undaunted, the purgees formed their own new, independent federation, changed its name to the Congress of Industrial Organizations to keep their acronym the same, and the flood gates of organization finally opened up.

All through the fall of 1936—the fall before the Woolworth's strike—CIO organizers fanned out into industrial communities in the Northeastern and Midwestern United States. The United Mine Workers (UMW) alone, led by the famous John L. Lewis, donated half a million dollars to build the Steel Workers' Organizing Committee (SWOC). Within a few months, over a hundred thousand steelworkers in a hundred and fifty different towns had rushed to join. Meanwhile, CIO organizers wove together a welter of small auto workers' unions into a new, unified body, the United Auto Workers (UAW). Throughout that fall, UAW members led small, sporadic strikes at parts plants and other factories in the upper Midwest, nothing huge, but December brought the first sign of what was about to come: UAW workers who made brakes at the Kelsey-Hayes plant in Detroit won a sit-down strike.

Then, suddenly and unexpectedly, the UAW took on General Motors, the largest corporation in the world. On December 30, 1936, in Flint, Michigan—about seventy miles outside Detroit—autoworkers staged a sit-down strike at the General Motors Fisher Body plant. The Flint strike, in turn, forced the company to stop production at other plants all over the country, idling 112,000 workers. Riveted, the nation watched for six weeks as the strikers camped out in the plant, the National Guard camped in the streets, the governor refused to send soldiers into the buildings, and local police and strikers battled it out with tear gas both inside and outside the plant. Finally, miraculously, on February 11, 1937, the mighty General Motors capitulated to the pipsqueak United Auto Workers and agreed to recognize the union and to negotiate wage increases and better working conditions. The nation was stunned. The greatest of corporations had been brought to its knees. Suddenly anything was possible.

For a few days local people absorbed the news. Then all hell broke loose in Detroit. In the second week after the General Motors settlement, four or five thousand working people at twenty or thirty different workplaces throughout the city went on strike. Some just walked out the old-fashioned way; others sat down. On Monday, February 22, for example, three hundred auto body workers at Briggs Manufacturing in Highland Park stopped work and occupied their plant. On Tuesday, thirty men who drove liquor trucks for the Star Transfer Lines struck and won their demands in a single day. On Wednesday, three hundred women and a handful of men who worked at the Ferry-Morse Seed company staged their own sit-down strike, and at the Conant Factory Lunch, sixty high school boys who delivered food to local factories sat down and after five hours won a pay raise from $1.00 to $1.25 an hour. That very night fifty-five charwomen who cleaned the Penobscot Building won a raise in pay after a two-hour work stoppage of their own.

The strikes and victories went on and on. On Thursday the Ferry-Morse Seed workers won their strike with a ten- to twenty-five-cent an hour pay increase and a forty-hour work week. At the Bon Dee Golf Ball Company, six workers sat down; workers at the Splendid Laundry announced they'd won a pay increase. At the Massachusetts Laundry, "300 girls sat down and demanded a straight ten cents an hour increase." Organizing worked.

Every day the women who worked at the downtown Detroit Woolworth's would have read about these events in the paper and heard about them on their radios. Every day they would have heard tales of daring actions from neighbors and friends, sisters and brothers, boyfriends, fathers, and mothers. Every day they would have had more time to think about the General Motors victory and all the subsequent gains workers in Detroit were winning with their strikes. And every day they would have wondered if they could do it too.

On Saturday morning they all showed up at work, in their tidily pressed uniforms and sleek dark skirts. They'd heard enough to make up their minds.

MANAGEMENT TO WOOLWORTH STRIKERS: DROP DEAD

Saturday, February 27, 11:30 A.M. Upstairs, in that all-important meeting, manager Frank Mayer had tried his sweet talk, but to no avail; the women had shouted back no. Now they were out on strike for real—they'd done it. But what came next?

First, and most urgently, they needed to secure the doors to make sure none of their fellow workers defected. Mayer had already rushed his own guards to the doors to keep new customers out.

Girl Strikers Occupy Chain Store, Win Big

Quickly the strikers and their allies from the waiters' union took over the doors from management and seized store keys from other employees—stock boys, waffling salesclerks—who remained. Within minutes "a huge crowd . . . gathered at the Woodward Avenue doors," reported the *Detroit Times*, "but nobody was admitted. Vigilant girl strikers guarded all doors."

That still left around two hundred "amazed" customers trapped inside the store. A few fled out the door immediately, but it soon became clear that most of them wanted to stay and watch the excitement. "The management sought to get the public out, but the customers wanted to remain and view a sit-down strike first hand," said the *Detroit News*. Woolworth's shoppers, after all, were themselves working-class men and women, conscious of the city's sit-down strikes of the previous weeks and perhaps quite sympathetic. Some of them might even have known the strike was about to happen and been in the store deliberately. Gradually, over the next hour, Mayer and the other managers hustled them out, a handful at a time.

Inside, it wasn't clear what would happen next. Curious faces started to press against the glass out front, so Mira Komaroff, from the waiters' and waitresses' union, organized a group of women to lower all the blinds and cover the street-level windows with brown wrapping paper from the store. Then they rolled out sheets of the same paper over the counters, covering the merchandise as the clerks always did at the end of the day.

From the very beginning, the occupiers started to enjoy themselves immensely—and that would prove a key to their power and solidarity during the strike. According to the *Detroit Free Press*, as the women left Mayer's office, they "laughed and shouted and paraded up and down the stairways in a noisy celebration." They mobbed the three pay phones at the back of the main floor to call their relatives and warn them excitedly that they might be in the store indefinitely, joking, "You better expect me when you see me." One large group settled down in little clusters on the stairs; others huddled at the counters and started playing checkers. Someone pulled out a deck of cards decorated with polka dots and a pair of little Scottie dogs on the back and started a game with three other women at the lunch counter.

But what, exactly, was going on? Would they be in the store for seven weeks, like the General Motors strikers in Flint? Or had they just signed up for a three-hour tour, like most of the Detroit workers who had staged quickie sit-downs the week before?

By noon the store was caught in a strangely suspended state: it was filled with food, all set up for the lunch rush. But the strikers carefully "kept away from the counters where food was spread out ready for the luncheon crowd." Instead, some of the women who'd brought bag lunches began to share them around, offering sandwiches and celery sticks, laughingly peeling bananas and feeding them to each other. At 1:30, Frank Mayer appeared at the top of the stairs and boomed, "Go downstairs and have lunch. It's on the house." The strikers cheered him and crowded to the counters, "where the piles of fruit and rows of pies disappeared quickly, adding to the good natured tone of the strike." Meanwhile the guards persuaded the last few customers to slip out the door.

All that food produced a rush of good feeling toward Frank Mayer. "To show their gratitude, they washed the dishes afterward," the *Detroit Free Press* reported. At this point Vita Terrall, the women's leader throughout the strike and the only individual striker the papers identified fully, began to speak directly to reporters. She was married, twenty-four years old, and worked at the candy counter. Terrall told the press after lunch that "they all like[d] Mayer and had 'nothing against him'"; the real battle, she said, was against the regional Woolworth's management in Cleveland. Floyd Loew, the organizer, had made the same argument to the strikers during lunch: "Your quarrel is not with the resident manager. . . . Stick by him. The quarrel is with the company." ("Loew's speech brought cheers between bites.")

Then suddenly the other shoe fell, and it all got very serious. Mayer was only the local store manager, and at 2:00 his boss, A. J.

Girl Strikers Occupy Chain Store, Win Big

Dahlquist, the district superintendent for Woolworth's forty stores in the Detroit area, showed up. Vita Terrall rounded everyone up onto the main stairwell between the first and second floors, the only place large enough for all to fit, for another meeting. Louis Koenig, business agent for the waiters' and waitresses' union, once again presented the strikers' official demands, this time to Dahlquist: a ten-cent an hour raise, union recognition, time and a half for overtime after forty-eight hours, no charge for uniforms or for their laundering, seniority rights within each department, free lunches for the soda fountain workers up to fifty cents a day, and all new employees to be hired through the union office. It was quite a list—note how the demands included monetary issues but also shorter hours of work and, very importantly, regulation of the employment process: a codified system of seniority to counter the capricious and often sexually insidious decisions of individual managers, and a regularized system of initial employment, in which Woolworth's management could hire only union members.

In reponse, Dahlquist told Koenig, the strikers, and their allies essentially to drop dead. He had spoken to the Woolworth's district manager, O. L. Gause, he said, on the phone in Cleveland, and had an ultimatum: "There will be no negotiation under any circumstances until the union organizers have left and the store is emptied. . . . The store must be turned back to us." Then he upped the ante: if the strikers didn't leave immediately, Woolworth's would lock out the workers at all its other thirty-nine stores in Detroit. "We will close every store in the city if necessary for an indefinite period."

Most amazingly, the strikers were completely undaunted. They greeted Dahlquist's ferocious and quite serious ultimatum "with some giggling, a modicum of jeering and great derisive shouting," according to the *Detroit News*. Vita Terrall then stepped forward. "If we leave here we are licked," she told the women. "We simply must remain in the store."

"Are you going to stick?" she asked.

"We'll stick!" they shouted back. "We'll stay until the cows come home," a few piped in. And once again the women erupted in the choruses of voice and song that would carry them through their whole strike. First they belted out "America" over and over again, in Dahlquist's face. Then they sang other "patriotic songs."

By this time word had spread across the city of what the Woolworth's strikers had done, and visitors from the Detroit labor movement began to join them on the stairs to express solidarity. (Dahlquist must eventually have slunk away). Bill Marshall, President of UAW Local 7 at the Chrysler plant showed up. So did Frances Comfort from the Detroit Federation of Teachers. "I was really thrilled when I heard what you cute kids had done," she told the strikers. "Some people say you're lawbreakers, but I'm here, a schoolteacher, proud to be among you. Many of you girls were in my classes in school and there you were trained to expect something from life." But here they were instead, she said, "working for a hopeless pay. . . . You are fighting not only for yourselves, but for thousands of girls like yourselves all over the country." It was all a spectacular ritual of solidarity, and enormous fun.

But Dahlquist's ultimatum had been a serious one. And it was now clear that this wasn't just a three-hour tour. Dahlquist agreed to meet on Sunday at 2:00 P.M. with Louis Koenig of the Waiters' and Waitresses' Union, plus representatives of the cooks' and retail clerks' unions—each of whom, in classic AFL fractional style, claimed jurisdiction over a different group of Woolworth's workers. That meant, at the very least, that the women would be in the store for the night and well into the next day. "Now the women's work was cut out for them," as Floyd Loew later put it.

FIVE AND DIME STRIKERS SETTLE IN FOR LONG STAY; UNION OFFICIALS RUSH IN

By the time the Woolworth's women had launched their strike, though, workers in the Detroit area, across the United States, and throughout Europe had fine-tuned the art of the sit-down strike. In a strike of any sort, the workers have a basic goal: to shut down the employer's business by withholding their labor. To do so, they need to keep their own ranks solid so that none of the workers returns to work, and they also need to prevent strikebreakers from getting in to do the job. In conventional strikes of the 1930s, workers tried to mount thick, raucous picket lines outside the workplace, both to keep scabs from entering and to shore up their own spirits. There was always the very concrete risk that employers would send in police, private security, or belligerent scabs to force their way through the picket line and reopen the workplace.

A sit-down strike offered multiple advantages over a conventional strike. First of all, scabs (managers today like to clean up their reputation by referring to them as "replacement workers") couldn't take over the jobs of the striking workers because the strikers were still right there, in the workplace. Moreover, employers would be less inclined to send in the police to force out the strikers because they'd then risk damaging their own property—that was part of the cleverness of a sit-down. And if they did drag people out of the workplace, they'd have to do so violently, producing unsavory publicity for the company. The strikers, meanwhile, didn't have to survive icy temperatures on the picket line (it dropped to twenty-six degrees in Detroit on February 27)—they were cozily ensconced inside, and if management decided to turn off the heat, well, that might mean more bad publicity, frozen pipes, or even dangerous fires. Labor activists had also discovered that sit-down strikes raised the morale of the strikers. Squished in together, rather than isolated at home or in small conversations on the picket line, the strikers' spirits rose and an enormous group feeling developed—precisely the sense of solidarity that working-class struggle is all about.

No one really knows when or where sit-down strikes were first invented. Frank Murphy, the pro-labor governor of Michigan at the time of the Woolworth's strike, claimed that masons for the pharaohs of Egypt used sit-downs to address grievances in the tomb-building industry. In 1715, workers hired to build the Rouen Cathedral in Lille, France, staged a sit-down strike. English textile workers tried it in 1817. Closer to home, in 1884, workers at the Jackson Brewery in Cincinnati barricaded themselves behind beer barrels for sixty-five hours. The Industrial Workers of the World (IWW) experimented with a sit-down strike in Schenectady, New York, in 1906.

Only in the mid-1930s, though, did the sit-down emerge as a popular and tremendously effective weapon for working people. In 1934, 1935 and 1936, miners in Yugoslavia, Hungary, Poland, Spain, Salonika, Wales, England, and France, all sat down. In May and June of 1936 almost one-fifth of all wage earners in French factories and stores staged sit-down strikes. Well aware of what their brothers and sisters were up to in Europe, U.S. unions soon began to experiment with the strategy of occupying workplaces, especially meatpacking and auto plants, where activists began to perfect the "quickie" sit-down, by which a short strike for modest demands could produce results in a matter of hours. In 1936 a total of 34,565 U.S. workers occupied their workplaces in seventy different strikes; most were less than a day long. All this meant a wealth of collective experience. By the end of February 1937, the Detroit labor movement in particular had refined its support systems, especially regarding the key logistics of food, bedding, and publicity.

In this explosive context the Woolworth's workers were experimenting with their own use of a sit-down strike, and feeling out how organized labor might aid them. According to one account, several of the strikers had been members of Local 705 of the waiters' and waitresses' union of Detroit before the strike; but another account of equal reliability reported that none had previously been union members. Whichever was the case, it's clear that the women initiated their actions entirely on their own, led, we can speculate, by their own Vita Terrall.

The women didn't, it turns out, just suddenly jump into action when Floyd Loew blew the whistle. The details are sketchy, but at some point on Friday morning—that is, the day before—a group of women had met with manager Frank Mayer and presented their demands. He reportedly "promised to comply with their demands as far as he could." Not satisfied, the women held a big meeting that Friday night, at which they formed themselves into a union. Again on Saturday morning they presented their demands to Mayer. Again he waffled, with a few promises of minor raises. It was then that they decided to sit down—even though, we can note, they'd already won a bit by simply organizing a union and presenting demands.

After the strike had commenced, Mayer whined duplicitously, "[It] came without warning. No one presented any demands to me formally." He conceded that "some of the girls spoke to me about laundry bills yesterday, and the store has agreed to shoulder this responsibility." He also claimed to have raised the waitresses' pay by a dollar a day, and announced magnanimously that new "girls starting to work today" would be "hired at 29 cents an hour rather than 28 cents." Of course that wouldn't help the strikers one whit; nor had Mayer put any of his offers in writing. "Sure we got a raise," wisecracked one striker. "What are we going to do with that—buy gum?"

At some time during the day on Friday, representatives of the Woolworth's workers had also paid a visit to the waiters' and waitresses' union (Local 705 of the Hotel Employees and Restaurant Employees' International Union, or HERE), in the nearby Lawyers' Building. "The Woolworth girls came to our offices with a list of demands and asked us to help get them," Mira Komaroff recalled. From that point onward and to the very end, staff members and rank-and-filers from Local 705 would play crucial roles in the Woolworth's strike.

Local 705 had three very distinct characters on its staff that day. The first, and oldest, was Louis Koenig, the secretary-treasurer of the local and very much the man in charge. Koenig (he pronounced it *Kerr*-nik), about forty-nine at the time, was a taciturn fellow who almost never smiled, hence his nickname "Smiley." Koenig had been born in Rohatyn, Austria, and had come to the United States when he was fifteen. He'd worked for a while as a waiter at the New York Stock Exchange Club and then become an officer of the Hotel Employees and Restaurant Employees' Union in New York. In 1916 Koenig moved to Detroit, where he and his pals working at the Detroit Athletic Club, almost all immigrant men from Europe, formed Local 705, the waiters' union. After four years as the local's president, Koenig moved into its leading staff position and was still there in 1937.

Koenig was a typical old-guard AFL business unionist. His local—and it was very much *his* local—represented around six hundred people in the mid-1930s, most of them waiters at the big downtown hotels and a few elite clubs. During the Prohibition era, Koenig had obtained most of the union's contracts by picketing, or threatening to picket, illegal bars and restaurants that served booze. If the cops showed up, the joints would be busted, so it was easier for employers to just sign with the union. Koenig's methods brought a few members into the local, but only from the top down. Rank-and-file members had little role or presence in the local, and he wanted it that way. Perhaps a dozen of its members were African American. They weren't allowed into the union's meetings at all. Known as the "Paradise Valley group," they had to meet separately in the basement.

Louis Koenig was never happy about allowing women into his union, either. In 1925, Local 705 had merged with a new Detroit waitresses' union, but twelve years later Koenig remained hostile to organizing women. "They get married and have babies," he was still complaining in 1972. "It's a devil of a job keeping up with them."

Koenig's attitude was classic. In the mid-1930s almost all the AFL unions were hostile to allowing women into the labor movement. Stereotypes abounded: women were flighty, only interested in marrying, only in the labor force temporarily; white-collar workers like secretaries and store clerks weren't real "workers" worthy of the labor movement. Some AFL unions, such as the building trades, machinists, and coal miners, actively kept women workers out of their unions and froze them out of employment in their fields altogether. Nonetheless, women workers constituted around 10 percent of all AFL members at the time. The vast majority of them were in the big garment workers' unions, in textile unions, or in scattered unions representing waitresses, laundry workers, and agricultural workers.

Would the rising CIO change all that? In February of 1937 it didn't necessarily look that way. After all, the big thrust of CIO organizing in the fall of 1936 had been in mass production: steel, autos, rubber, and electrical manufacturing. Except for the latter, workers in these fields were almost entirely male; so were the hundreds of activists who had gone out to organize them. Because the CIO explicitly committed itself to the whole-industry organizing principle rather than craft-by-craft jurisdictions, in theory it would embrace all unskilled workers and therefore would help organize women. But in practice almost all its energy so far had gone into organizing men. When the UAW had so spectacularly organized General Motors in the Flint sit-down strike that winter, it had banned GM's female clerical workers from joining the union.

For all his hostility to women unionists, Louis Koenig saw the handwriting on the restaurant walls. In 1933, he met a politically passionate young woman, Mira Komaroff, and offered her a job on his union's staff. At first he only let her work as a secretary, but soon she was off organizing female hotel and restaurant workers as well as men, and eventually Koenig was referring to Komaroff as his protégée.

By all accounts, Mira Komaroff had a spectacular personality: she was energetic, sharp as a tack, and could charm just about anybody—the kind of woman that writers of the time described as "vivacious" and a "firebrand." Thirty years after her death, people who knew her, whatever they thought of her politics, still get an admiring grin on their faces at the mention of her name; she had a rare, special charisma. In photographs she smiles right into the camera and decades later looks as though she could walk right out of the picture and talk you into anything.

Mira Komaroff was twenty-three in February of 1937. She came from a middle-class Detroit family; her dad sold insurance and real estate. She'd attended Carnegie Tech in Pittsburgh for a year, studying interior design, but had to drop out as the family's finances shriveled with the Great Depression. So she came back to Detroit and jumped into labor and left-wing politics. In the middle years of the Depression—1933–35—Mira belonged to the Proletarian Party, a Marxist group that had split off from the Socialist Party in 1919. The Proletarian Party was famous for its educational activities—soapbox speakers, public meetings, and monthly study groups for its members, which Mira attended regularly. Through the party Mira deepened her understanding of class relationships in the United States and of the need for working-class self-organization. She quickly became a key figure in Louis Koenig's Local 705, working to expand the union in downtown Detroit hotels and restaurants.

Then Floyd Loew showed up, and Mira was not happy about it. Loew was older—about thirty-five in 1937—a "tough, muscular" guy who allegedly "could talk as effectively as he could use his fists." (One union dissident later alleged that Loew had pushed him down a flight of stairs at the local's office.) Loew had grown up as a poor Michigan farm boy and then worked his way around the country as a waiter, becoming active in Hotel and Restaurant locals in Los Angeles and Miami. He came to Detroit in 1935, where he got a job waiting tables on the breakfast shift at the Book-Cadillac Hotel, and he too got involved with the Proletarian Party. In early 1936, Koenig hired Loew as an organizer. By all accounts, he was a great organizer—aggressive, energetic, and persuasive (but not "vivacious"— men never got to be "vivacious").

Mira Komaroff was deeply threatened by Floyd Loew. He was on her turf, he was outshining her, he was older, and he was a man.

In late 1936 Koenig gave him a big raise; now he made more money than she did. Komaroff, meanwhile, had been offered a job by Governor Frank Murphy, with the Michigan Employment Security Commission; by early 1937 she was working full-time at the commission and only organizing for Local 705 at night and on the weekends.

Throughout January and early February, Loew, Komaroff, and Max Gazan, of the local cooks' union, had all worked together supporting the Flint General Motors sit-down strike. Once again the gender politics had gotten a bit thick. In the first days of the massive strike, autoworkers' wives had set up soup kitchens to feed the hundreds of strikers inside the plant. They were overwhelmed with work, so the UAW called on the cooks' and waiters' unions for help. "We'll take care of it," Loew offered. "But tell the women to pick up their damn pots and pans and clear the hell out of here." This does not suggest that Loew would have been entirely respectful of the female strikers at Woolworth's—or of Komaroff.

Certainly, though, Koenig, Komaroff, and Loew each brought crucial assets to the Woolworth's workers. For one thing, their organization legitimated the strike. The strikers were now supported by an established union, with officers and everything, part of the larger Hotel Employees and Restaurant Employees' International Union, a national body. (By AFL jurisdictional etiquette, however, the clerks would be assigned to the retail clerks' union if the strike succeeded, even though that union played only a token role in helping them.) All three staffers from the waiters' and waitresses' union had highly developed negotiating skills, and they quickly took over that end of the strike—it was Koenig, not Vita Terrall, who presented the women's demands to Dahlquist on the stairwell; it was Koenig, plus male officials from the cooks' and retail clerks' unions, who arranged to meet with the managers on Sunday. Finally, both Komaroff and Loew had experience with the complex logistical details of figuring out how over a hundred people could eat, drink, and sleep over in a five-and-dime store with only a few hours' notice. That didn't necessarily mean they entirely knew what they were doing. "It was a real grass root [*sic*] movement and we were really green and . . . almost got run over," Loew recalled fifty years later. "We were all new and without experience."

For the most part we can only speculate about the concrete interactions and negotiations between the strikers and the organizers. We do know that before they broke up their raucous meeting on the stairwell that Saturday afternoon, the Woolworth's strikers began to organize themselves internally, with help, evidently, from Loew and Komaroff. They elected Vita Terrall as Strike Committee chair and then formed themselves into seven other committees: Food, Store Clean-up, Sales, Health, Cheer-up, Entertainment, and Scrapbook.

Immediately the women sent word out to their families and friends that they needed mattresses and blankets. In mid-afternoon, Koenig and Charles Paulsen, from the cook's union, arrived with a truckload of mattresses, and the remaining strikers who hadn't volunteered for any committee now formed a Bed Committee to carry them. The mattresses were the old kind, of blue-and-green jacquard fabric with big white floral designs and thick-stitched borders. Tugging and pulling, the strikers splayed them out along the first floor aisles, sideways, just barely fitting, so the women's heads and toes were almost up against the counters. They'd have to sleep three to a mattress; each got her own brightly colored plaid or striped blanket.

The women spent the rest of the afternoon perfecting the whole layout and, once again, partying hard. "Radios blared . . . and the clerks and fountain girls celebrated their own daring by dancing in the aisles." Various friends passed cigarettes into the store, and the women set up a smoking section in the basement, which had a tiled floor. They mobbed the phones once again, and again took up cards, checkers, and singing—all the while posing for photographs, sometimes exuberantly, sometimes coyly, and sometimes with a look of giggling astonishment at what they had done.

[88]

Girl Strikers Occupy Chain Store, Win Big

Dinner was once again on the house, Mayer offered, so they ate up the ice cream, hot dogs, and piles of jelly donuts arrayed on polished metal pedestals atop the counters. Mira announced that 11:00 P.M. would be curfew time. Slowly the chaos settled down. All the men in the store left, except for Floyd Loew, the union organizer, and Frank Mayer, the store manager, who dragged cots upstairs. Mira stayed too, downstairs. The women gradually giggled and whispered themselves to sleep. These were very young women, many of whom had never spent the night away from home before, and they were, after all, lying in the dark on the cold wooden floor of a four-story variety store.

Suddenly someone let out a scream, and then more screams spread across the store. A rat had jumped onto one of the mattresses, and in its own panic at the first screech began leaping across mattress after mattress, trying to escape. Panic broke out. Many of the women were ready to leave right then and there. But a quick huddle among Floyd, Mira, Vita, and a few others produced a solution: the women dragged their mattresses up to the second floor, where, in theory, rats would fear to tread, since there was no food on that level. Finally they all settled down—rats, strikers, organizers, and the boss—and the first day of the Woolworth's strike was over.

CANARIES JOIN SONG RAISED BY WOOLWORTH GIRLS
AS PRIMPING REPLACES CLERKING

Sunday, February 28. Curfew lifted at 8 A.M. The strikers crawled out of bed, got out their compacts, put on their makeup, and prepared for the reporters who, they knew, were about to rush in. "We had plenty of mattresses, blankets, and pillows and all of us slept well," Vita Terrall told the press.

Saturday had been dramatic, to say the least, and lots of fun amidst all the confrontation, but now the women settled into a daily routine. Now the committee structure kicked in. Now their friends came by and slipped them nightgowns, toothpaste, more blankets,

[89]

cosmetic cases, and more cigarettes, which the women piled up on the counters in the basement. Floyd and Mira warned the strikers not to touch a thing that belonged to the store, but they seemed to have touched quite a lot, even if the counters were carefully covered with the brown wrapping paper. All those useful objects for which Woolworth's was so famous became, well, useful; the novelty items, lots of fun. The Sales Committee carefully kept track of it all: the strikers didn't steal or hurt anything, they just did a little shopping.

The Health Committee had a bit of work to do, too. Within the first twenty-four hours there was a run on "headache tablets." Reporters also noted, somewhat intrusively, that the change in the women's diet caused constipation, so someone brought in a supply of mineral oil and the women were all required to swallow a big spoonful every morning, under the supervision of a physician who showed up every day. The women joined in daily sit-ups and other calisthenics, too.

They also tightened up the food logistics. On Sunday morning, the strikers kicked out the manager for good, and took over the food operations themselves. From now on volunteers from the cook's union, coordinated by Floyd Loew, prepared their food in a kitchen set up outside, then carried it in to the lunch counter in the basement, where the women served each other. The strikers, after all, included waitresses, bakery assistants, and cooks. Some of the food they prepared themselves in the store's own kitchen. It was all brilliantly convenient. At Woolworth's—in contrast to those famous strikes in automobile factories—the women had a kitchen, cleaning supplies, headache tablets, safety pins, plus bathrooms and a candy counter all right there.

They set up systems for daily maintenance too: the Clean-up Committee swept floors, washed counters, and watched for rats. One group of women took care of feeding the canaries and cleaning their cages in the basement. As time passed, some of the strikers started washing clothes in the store's various sinks and hung them out to dry on the fire escape. In other words, they made themselves at home.

All this time they stayed in close contact with their friends and families, sweethearts and husbands through constant phone calls on the store's three phones and furtive contacts through the front door. The situation was clearly stressful for some or the women wouldn't have formed their Cheer-up Committee. "This committee served as a very important committee," Floyd Loew later wrote, "because most of the young women still lived at home and this endeavor was an overwhelming experience for such young participants." In another memoir, he recalled, "The Cheer-up Committee was made up of a smiling and bubbly bunch of women and they were really needed. They watched for the first curling lip and they soon had all sadness chased away."

All in all, though, the strikers were still having a great time. A Pathé Newsreels team that showed up Sunday commented with a bit of puzzlement, "They seem to enjoy themselves despite the troubled atmosphere." These young women were used to working six days a week, nine hours a day, standing on their feet the entire time. All of a sudden they not only had the day off, but they could play all they wanted. By that morning they had changed into sensible shoes, T-shirts, and pants.

Some of the women played with the canaries; some of them gathered in small groups and played cards and checkers. Two women in loud plaid playsuits with matching square caps slid down the banisters, over and over. Dozens sat on the main stairwell and took up knitting, crotcheting, and embroidery, utilizing the second floor's cornucopia of embroidery hoops, knitting needles, and skeins of yarn.

The women moved in on the sheet music department, too, and sang on the stairs for hours and hours. (A newsreel captures them swaying back and forth on the stairs, singing, one playing a mandolin, another holding, mysteriously, a toilet plunger.) A favorite, which they sang over and over again, was "Hail, hail, the gang's all here." They also liked "Pennies from Heaven" and rewrote a verse of "John Brown's Body" as "We'll hang old Woolworth to a sour apple tree." Another favorite was "Mademoiselle from Armentieres," to which they made up their own words:

> Sit down girls, sit down girls,
> Parlez-vous.
> Sit down girls, come sit down, don't be afraid to [stand your ground?].
> Hinky dinky parlez-vous.

Someone hauled in a Victrola; records appeared. Radios blared. They danced in couples. The Entertainment Committee organized "impromptu entertainments" (what they were exactly we'll just have to leave up to our imaginations). And they arranged for the musicians' union to show up nightly for free concerts, to which they also danced.

We know much of this because much of it took place in front of dozens of reporters—not just those faces pressed to the glass out front, but *Life* magazine, famous national radio broadcaster H. V. Kaltenborn, the *Chicago Tribune*, the *New York Times*, the *Daily Worker*, *Women's Wear Daily*, Pathé Newsreels, and three daily and one weekly newspaper from Detroit, among others.

The media world rushed in, but what did it see? Kaltenborn, the radio man, loved the strike: "The CIO unions might want to take lessons from the Five-and-Ten cent crew on strike strategy," he told the nation. For Kaltenborn, the strike was a serious demonstration of how to build a powerful labor movement.

But for almost all the other reporters the occupation was anything but serious. Rather it offered an opportunity to trivialize the women as silly girls playing strike and to titillate readers with their alleged obsession with beauty and boys. Every single report described the strikers as "girls," never as women, although most were over the age of eighteen, and many were in their twenties, thirties, or forties. Their gender was always identified; they were always "girl strikers," unlike the General Motors sit-downers, for example, who were "striking workers," and almost never "boys" except very rarely in a jovial, comradely sense. Even the Communist Party's *Daily Worker* couldn't resist referring to the women's hair color and body type: "Young girls, blonde, brunette, slim, plump, going on strike for their rights."

Life magazine, in a big, four-page photo spread published after the strike was over, cast it as "Camp Woolworth": "The newest type of camping excursion is attended not by children of the rich but by members of the working classes. . . . Youngest, prettiest, most prevailingly feminine of such recent 'campers' were the 110 girls in Detroit's main Woolworth store who went on strike Feb. 27." The story continued with cute references to "camp duties," "camp equipment," and a "sit-down picnic" in Woolworth's "camping ground."

In account after account, the strikers were alleged to be obsessed with beauty. "Night and day one hundred girls occupy the closed store and primping replaces clerking," intoned Pathé Newsreels. The strikers, the press noted, had set up their own beauty parlor in a corner of the store: "Everyone got a manicure and finger wave." *Life* assured, "A good appearance is maintained by Woolworth girls who comb their hair in the women's rest room and do not allow their camping excursion to interfere with their prinking [preening]."

The women were also supposed to be obsessed with boyfriends. The strike started on a Saturday, offering reporters the opportunity to focus on the all-important Saturday night date as a threat to working-class solidarity. "Many girls wanted to leave the store because of a 'date with the boy friend,'" reported the *Detroit Times*. "These requests Miss Terral [*sic*] refused." A reporter for the *Detroit News* did a little eavesdropping on Saturday afternoon. "'Gosh, I've got a date with my boy friend,'" a dark-haired girl named Mazie supposedly worried. "'I can't reach him by telephone, either. He's going to think I'm standing him up.'"

These all-important dates allegedly produced the strike's only reported deserters. According to the *Detroit News,* "The first sign of any defection came at 3 P.M.," when Vita Terrall "discovered half a dozen girls deserted to keep Saturday night dates. They got out of the building through a basement door, through the assistance of two stock room boys, who were not on strike."

It's impossible to distinguish between what the Woolworth's strikers actually did and thought and how they were depicted. Clearly some of them were sincerely concerned about dates; but we only know that because reporters repeatedly brought the question up. We don't know if any of the Flint workers, for example, were just as worried about their own dates. We do know that the Woolworth's strikers themselves, on their second or third day, set up a "Love Booth." Boyfriends could enter the store and inhabit the booth for five minutes with their sweeties. (We are left imagining exactly what the couples might have accomplished in precisely five minutes.)

A favorite angle in the press was a little book called *How to Get Your Man and Hold Him,* with which, they insisted, the strikers were obsessed. A *Detroit News* photographer captured four women propped up on their stomachs on the floral-patterned mattresses, each reading a copy in what was clearly a posed shot. The *Detroit Times* reported that "a little huddle in one corner" had snatched up the book. "The girl who held the book was surrounded by others who pored over her shoulders and under her arms, intent on solving the problem." *Life* caught a photo of a huge, just unwrapped pile of over two hundred copies of the book—offering "Secrets of Flattery" for only ten cents—but conceded that "most of [the women] are sufficiently good-looking to make scholarly study of romantic technique unnecessary." One account claimed that the strikers had requested that the union buy them all copies, but it seems more plausible that Woolworth's simply had a large quantity in supply that day—another cheap, useful item.

In the media's eyes, then, the Woolworth's strikers were like Barbara Hutton: obsessed with beauty, makeup, hair, and fashion, and eager to parlay all four, along with a big dose of sparkle and flattery, to capture the man of their choice.

But of course it was all more complicated than that. The strikers were quite capable of manipulating the media right back. They were the ones who called Pathé Newsreels to come film them in the first place. The sleek somber skirts and dressy, formal lace collars the clerks are wearing in press photos from Saturday might have been their regular work clothes, or the strikers may have dressed to the nines that morning, knowing full well they were about to be photographed by every paper in town. They definitely didn't wear high heels on normal work days. Once on strike the women read newspapers voraciously; discarded papers piled up in mountains in the aisles. The newspapers, in turn, ran photos of the strikers lined up at the lunch counter reading about themselves in the very same papers. The strikers were so conscious of the role of the media that one of the very first committees they set up was the Scrapbook Committee, to save all those stories about themselves. In other words, the women were both aware of media attention and able to employ it for their own ends, in part to buoy their spirits in what was, after all, a dicey situation.

Ironically, the "silly girls playing strike" media pitch gave the strikers power. It kept them on the front pages of the papers for days on end. Their very innocence legitimated their struggle. If these were just silly girls, why should Woolworth's exploit them? And if these were boy-crazy young things, just having a bit of fun in the aisles, it would certainly not look good at all if Woolworth's sent in the National Guard or thugs to drag them out by their carefully coiffed hair. Being cast as silly and a little stupid, in other words, protected them.

Being white girls protected them, too. Imagine the response if the strikers had been African American. Media sympathy for their plight as oppressed workers wouldn't have been in place beforehand—no Bing Crosby crooning hit songs that built up sympathy. Once on strike, police and public tolerance for their lawbreaking behavior would have been zero. Media interest outside the African American press would be mostly nonexistent or hostile. And *Life* would certainly not have shown up to depict them playing at Camp Woolworth.

If the Woolworth strikers' whiteness and their supposed silliness protected them, equally importantly, their beauty culture wasn't stupid at all. They knew that it was useful to powder their noses and put on a bit of lipstick before the reporters rushed in the door on Sunday morning. They took pleasure in making each other up and in looking good—that was why they set up a beauty parlor in the store. Photographs of the last day of their strike show them glowing, almost all with a set of beautiful curls, a bow in their hair, and a corsage, which, we can suspect, they had crafted from materials in the store during their occupation. Historian Kathy Peiss, in her wonderful study *Hope in a Jar,* has shown how savvy and artful working-class women were in their use of cosmetics. Women, she writes, deployed makeup "to declare themselves—to announce their adult status, sexual allure, youthful spirit, political beliefs— and even to proclaim the *right* to self-definition." Boys and sex could be fun, too. There was nothing wrong with wanting to go out on Saturday night for a kiss, a few well-placed squeezes, or maybe a lot more. And some of the women were in fact married.

"Getting a man and holding him" was in fact a smart economic strategy. Think about it: these were young working-class women in the depths of the Great Depression. What were their choices? Stay single, stay in the labor force, join a union, go on strike, better their wages and working conditions—O.K., they were doing that. Or they could find a young man with a steady job and good wages, and marry him. In many ways that was the best choice available, and they knew it. They also knew that statistically, their chances of marriage had gotten slimmer and slimmer during the Depression. "We have no money to get married," one Woolworth clerk told a New York interviewer in 1939. "Unless Lady Luck comes along, we never will."

Girl Strikers Occupy Chain Store, Win Big

The very first page of *How to Get Your Man and Hold Him* only confirmed their choices: "No nice girl admits it out loud, but it is nevertheless true that there comes a time in every girl's life when she is seized with an urge to get married." The cause could be "strictly biological," or the urge could be caused by a Clark Gable movie, the author speculated, but it could also be caused by:

(a) The sudden realization that spinsterhood is just around the corner.
(b) The struggle to make both ends meet on one under-nourished pay envelope.
(c) Being fed up with the monotonous business of punching a time clock and writing letters.

Given the alternatives, in other words, it was smart to keep that date. Mazie needed to make that phone call or her boyfriend might think she was standing him up; she needed to paint her nails, or he might do a little shopping around himself.

Because they weren't, in fact, Barbara Hutton. She was rich, they were poor. She was rich *because* they were poor. These young women needed men for enormous economic reasons; Barbara Hutton had millions of her own and could buy a man by crooking her glittering little finger in his direction.

In their reports on the strike, labor and left-wing publications jumped on the contrast. The *Michigan Labor Paper* headlined an editorial "The Countess and the Counter Girl." The *Daily Worker,* in a story on the strike, ran a photograph not of the strikers themselves, but of Barbara Hutton. Best of all, the Woolworth's strikers made up wonderful songs about Hutton, and the press repeated them:

> Barbara Hutton's got the dough, parlez vous.
> We know where she got it, too, parlez vous.
> We slave at Woolworth's five-and-dime,
> The pay we get is sure a crime.
> Hinky dinky parlez vous.

Some of the women working at Woolworth's that first morning may have decided hanging on to their man was in fact more important than striking—hence the basement-door deserters, although there were plenty of other reasons for skipping out. But the majority of the women tried to mediate between the two strategies, to make striking and seducing compatible. "Sure I love you," one striker assures someone on the phone in a newsreel, "but we're sticking right here until we win." We don't really know: maybe their sweeties were militant union activists who loved them all the more because they were on strike.

Many of the strikers leapt to enforce solidarity among the ranks lest their sisters waver. Not only did Vita Terrall police the doors, but on that Saturday night, when "some of the girls thought of their dates and tried to get out," according to the *Detroit News,* "Mae, of the sodas . . . just stuck her gum in the locks on the back doors. Those doors are locked for keeps." When Mazie, quoted earlier, allegedly lamented she couldn't get ahold of her boyfriend, " 'Forget it,' said her blond next-door neighbor, Sally. 'Don't you suppose he'll hear about this? . . . And anyhow . . . this is more important than your boyfriend. We've got to win this strike.' "

Defections aside, the women's beauty culture could also support their sense of community and solidarity. They had a lot of time to kill; they could bond by sharing tips on curling irons and clever flattery; they could keep themselves distracted by making out with boyfriends in that Love Booth; they could imagine a happy married future . . . and not worry about what the outcome of their strike might be.

In the rare instances we have in which the Woolworth's strikers spoke to the public directly, they didn't mention beautification at all but articulated the concrete reasons for their sit-down. "All we want is a living wage," they said, in big red crayon letters on pieces of cardboard and brown wrapping paper they put in the front windows facing the street. In Pathé's first newsreel of the strike, a woman in her twenties with brown hair, carefully pencilled arched eyebrows, glossy lipstick, and a striped cotton top says to the camera, very seriously: "We have the best food that anyone could ask for, and when we get our union, we hope that it will be recognized throughout all the retail stores so as to give us shorter hours and living wages. I thank you." She made a little bow, and smiled. She was probably Vita Terrall.

And there were other ways to resolve the contradiction between striking and seducing. The Love Booth aside, the strikers were, after all, having a great time without men. Once Loew and Mayer moved upstairs, the strike was one big endless all-female slumber party of indeterminate duration. The women did each other's nails and hair with loving affection and danced with their arms around each other's waists. If you watch Pathé's first newsreel carefully, you can catch one of the strikers reaching over to tickle the back of the woman next to her.

Sunday night, they tucked themselves in and dreamed sugary dreams of sweethearts, Barbara Hutton, and a living wage.

WOOLWORTH STRIKE ESCALATES
AS UNIONS CLOSE SECOND STORE

The strikers were having a great time, but the purpose of their strike wasn't to guarantee they had lots of fun; the goal, after all, was to get Woolworth's management to give in on wages, hours of work, and a sea of other demands. While all that dancing was going on on Sunday, the situation hadn't moved toward a resolution one whit. By Monday, March 1, two days had passed and Woolworth's hadn't budged an inch.

So on Monday, the unions escalated the situation dramatically, heightening the pressure on the Woolworth's managers and raising the stakes for everyone involved.

On Saturday afternoon, Louis Koenig had evidently threatened to close all forty Woolworth stores in Detroit, with their 1,000 employees. A bluff, maybe? Sometime on Monday in the morning or early afternoon, officials of the cooks', waiters', and retail clerks' unions had a private meeting downtown. Then, at 3:00, Mira Komaroff and other folks from the three unions drove down Woodward Avenue to a second, smaller Woolworth's store at 6565 Grand Boulevard, just off Woodward. They met briefly with a few of the twenty-six women who worked as clerks and waitresses there. At 3:30 sharp, Mira yelled out, "Strike! Strike!" and eleven women stopped working. "There was no disorder as the clerks who did not desire to participate donned wraps and left," reported the *Daily Worker.* "The striking girls clustered about the soda fountain, talking with the union organizers. Customers departed, doors were locked." Mira and the other officials bought "a supply of food at the lunch counter with which to feed the strikers." Then they asked all the managers to leave. "There was no violence," reported the *Detroit Times,* once again. And now a second Woolworth's store was occupied by striking women.

Now the unions' threats to escalate the strike to all forty stores in Detroit looked a whole lot more serious. Monday night, Louis Koenig cast his own ultimatum back at Woolworth's, upping the ante still further: "Unless the strike here is settled within a week of the time it started [i.e., by Saturday, March 6]," he proclaimed, "I will ask the executive council of our association to call a national sit-down"—thus closing all the Woolworth's stores in the country.

Local solidarity in support of the strikers at both stores shot up. A formal system of picketing outside kicked in. During the next few days "nearly every hotel worker in the downtown area found their way to the Woolworth store to wish the women luck," Loew recalled. One visitor was Paul Domeney, an immigrant from Transylvania who worked as a room service waiter at the Book-Cadillac luxury hotel in downtown Detroit at the time, and was active as a leftist within the waiters' union. Together with Mira Komaroff he visited the picket line and even went inside the store to talk with the strikers and help shore up their spirits. Homer Martin, national president of the United Auto Workers, came in and gave a big pep talk, pledging his union's ongoing support.

Girl Strikers Occupy Chain Store, Win Big

Local Detroit activists like Paul Domeney, Mira Komaroff, and Floyd Loew assiduously sought to evade the growing national split between the jurassic AFL and the upstart CIO. While conflict between the two titans turned increasingly nasty on the national level, unionists on the ground in Detroit tried hard to keep working together in the interests of solidarity. "Our unions are AFL affiliates but we are working peaceably with [the] CIO," Mira Komaroff went out of her way to insist to the press. The waiters' and waitresses' union, affiliated nationally with the Hotel Employees and Restaurant Employees' International Union was, on the one hand, still an AFL union, as were the retail clerks. The United Auto Workers, on the other hand, was the quintessential CIO affiliate, challenging AFL craft jurisdictions as handily as it had taken on General Motors. Frank Martel, president of the Detroit and Wayne County Federation of Labor, emerged as a rare figure in this period, trying to bridge the gap between CIO and AFL. He not only showed up at the Woolworth's strike downtown the minute it broke out, but on Monday carefully told the press that "the local Federation would have been inadequate to handle the appeals of strikers had not the automobile union lent assistance."

Throughout the country, unions, working people, and their allies rushed to express their support for the Woolworth's strikers. Edward Flore, national president of HERE, announced that he would arrive in Detroit on the next Monday, March 8. Telegrams flooded in from Chicago, Philadelphia, Boston, New York, and all over, both to the Woolworth's strikers directly and to the national offices of HERE and the retail clerks' union. Someone named W. J. Boenckleman, from New Orleans, sent a telegram saying he held thirty shares of Woolworth's stock and was "100% with the sit-downers in their efforts to enforce demands." The strikers plastered their telegrams all over the store's ground-floor windows for all to see.

Supporters also sent cash to support the strikers, who needed money for food, supplies, and to replace the earnings they were forgoing with every passing day. Vita Terrall announced on Monday that the AFL had donated $1,000. Union staffers assured the press that the strikers had been guaranteed enough funds "to continue the strike indefinitely," with money promised from Chicago, New York, and other cities.

The unions did everything they could to publicize all this support, to signal to Woolworth's that they were invincible. But at the same time, in private, they were doing everything they could to create a way out for the corporation by setting up possible avenues for mediation. Throughout Monday and Tuesday rumors floated all over town that either the Detroit Board of Commerce or the Detroit Retail Merchants Association would be mediating a settlement.

But for all that, Woolworth's didn't move—or so it seemed.

Think about the situation from Woolworth's point of view. Its managers were caught between a rock of solidarity and a very expensive place. Unlike the "girls," they were not happy campers, and with every passing play day, they got less happy.

Who exactly was "Woolworth's" anyway? Ultimately, the corporation rested in the hands of its stockholders who, in 1937, included Frank Woolworth's heirs, the company's longtime upper-level managers and their heirs, and those who had bought its stock in later decades. In practice, an elaborate chain of command stretched upward and outward from local managers like Frank Mayer. When the strike started on Saturday morning, Mayer called his own boss, Dahlquist, the Detroit area manager—the man who issued the ultimatum at the top of the stairs that afternoon. Dahlquist, in turn, had called O. L. Gause, of Woolworth's regional headquarters in Cleveland. But even Gause wasn't really in charge; he then answered to the executives in the Woolworth's building in New York City. All these men—and they were all men—answered to Charles Deyo, the company's president.

The very elaborateness and length of this chain of command, combined with the firm's geographic dispersal in an era of expensive long-distance phone calls, slowed down the negotiation process immensely. This was no quickie, no three-hour tour, unlike so many of the dozens of sit-down strikes in Detroit the week before, in part because it took more than three hours for communication to move up, let alone back down, the chain of command.

The big shots in New York did everything they could to act like indifferent power figures at an omnipotent corporation swatting away the Detroit sit-downers like pesky flies. On Monday, after the occupation of the second store began, Edward P. Houbert, a lawyer for the company, insisted, "Our attitude is still the same—we will not bargain, as long as strikers remain in the stores." Company vice president E. C. Mauchly "telegraphed from New York that the strike was a local incident and would have to be handled through the district headquarters at Cleveland," *Women's Wear Daily* reported.

But Woolworth's bigness also meant that the stakes were higher. If the company gave in and granted the strikers' demands, it would cost a lot of money—not just in wages at the two stores on strike, but in the other forty Detroit stores as well. The stores' profits would drop and perhaps the company's stock price would plummet as well.

The managers had no way of knowing, moreover, if a small—but very very public—settlement with the unions in Detroit would lead to organizing efforts and sit-down strikes at their stores all over the country, or even in Canada, Great Britain, Germany, or Cuba. More broadly, they would have been deeply hostile, ideologically, to unions, especially the militant kind that occupied their property and held them hostage. They had a stake in drawing the line against the national upsurge of union activism under way, and some among them might even have been a little bit worried about a social revolution.

Much as it might have wanted to uphold their own version of corporate class solidarity during the Depression, Woolworth's also had to keep looking over its shoulder at its competitors. A settlement might disrupt its position in relation to other variety stores snapping at the heels of its market share, in particular S. S. Kresge—headquartered, coincidentally, in Detroit. Kresge itself, watching the sit-down handwriting on its own wall that Saturday, raised the wages of its own Detroit workers from $14 to $17 a week within five *hours* of the Woolworth's strike. Kresge's thus cleverly averted any labor action in its own stores, plus it enjoyed the nice side benefit of being open while Woolworth's was closed.

Last but not least, the public relations pressures on Woolworth's were enormous. The movement against "the chain store menace" was at its peak. It was the Great Depression, and here was a giant corporation exploiting innocent young white women. And of course, with their songs and pickets the strikers themselves kept reminding the public of the self-indulgent Barbara Hutton. Polls revealed that public opinion largely supported the new sit-down strikes. Working-class people were especially enthusiastic. And they shopped at Woolworth's—or at least they had before the strike.

Woolworth's had three basic choices: one, settle; two, hold out and see if the strikers would give up; or three, send in the police. The armed solution was a real option. All the company had to do was get a judge to issue an injunction against the strikers on trespassing charges and in theory it would be able to call upon the Detroit police or the National Guard to evict the strikers forcibly. That same Saturday another strike had erupted at the Ferro Stamping Company in Detroit, and by Tuesday its owners had obtained an injunction. The strikers had left the plant voluntarily, defeated. But not all judges would comply, and for a brief time in February and March, both the mayor of Detroit and Governor Frank Murphy were unwilling to send in troops to evict sit-downers—that was one reason why the General Motors strikers had won. The *Detroit Free Press* reported on Sunday that A. J. Dahlquist had "indicated that police action to gain evacuation was contemplated," but it seems to have been an empty threat. We have no other evidence that Woolworth's ever considered a forcible solution. Again, to do so would have been a spectacular public relations fiasco; all those nasty cops, all those manicured nails.

Clearly the strikers, when lined up in solidarity with all their allies all over the country, held enormous power over the corporation. Notice just one detail: when the women occupying the second store asked their own bosses to leave the store, the men filed out like obedient sheep.

But that didn't mean victory. It just meant that Woolworth's was feeling the heat.

SIT-DOWNS SPREAD IN AREA HOTELS;
WILL SEND FUNDS, SAY NEW YORK UNIONS

Tuesday, March 2. Day four of the Woolworth's strike. National solidarity ratcheted up another big notch. The executive committee of the big, radical Local #1250 of the Retail Clerks' International Protective Association in New York met that night, then dispatched a telegram of ringing support: "Congratulations courageous Woolworth workers. Notify us how we can cooperate." They had already planned a big dance for the coming Saturday night at the Savoy Ballroom, at 140th and Lenox Avenue, to benefit the Loyalist cause in the Spanish Civil War. On Tuesday night they voted to donate 25 percent of the take to their sisters in Detroit. Most importantly, the union was planning a demonstration for that same Saturday, March 6, which, it announced in a national press release, "will open a boycott of the Woolworth stores in New York pending the outcome of the strike." To keep the pressure on, a delegation from several local unions would call on Woolworth executives to notify them officially of the planned boycott and "urge granting of the Detroit demands." Hinting at future direct action of their own, the retail clerks' union also issued a statement that working conditions in New York City "were as bad or worse than those in Detroit."

By now people all over the country had been following the story for days. The papers had headlined the story since Saturday, the newsreels were now in the movie theaters, and regular working folks had had time to think about what the women were doing. The Communist Party's *Daily Worker,* based in New York, sent reporter Louise Mitchell out to check on what local Woolworth's workers had to say about their sisters in Detroit. "The slight, undernourished counter girl in a crisp white collar" who worked at the "wash cloth counter" confided, "Everyone is talking about it. . . . Everyone who comes in. . . . There's something going on all right." She was no dummy about cause and effect, either: "Everybody is sitting down. If you want something you just take a squat and they come to terms." At a different variety store, "over the sandwich counter," "a fair platinum haired girl" told Mitchell, "I'd like to sit right down now and do I wish I was there. If we ever did it in New York . . . they'd have a job to combat it." The "girl" behind the stationery counter agreed: "Wait till this thing comes to New York. Of course it'll come. We're all watching them and not saying much."

Closer to home, the lid burst off the top of labor activism in Detroit. Thousands of local workers had also had a few days to contemplate what the Woolworth's women were doing and be inspired themselves. Now service workers in downtown Detroit as well as factory workers suddenly sat down. Tuesday, at Stouffer's, sixty waitresses and kitchen workers occupied their restaurant at the middle of the lunchtime rush. Workers at Huyler's Cafeteria in the Fisher Building sat down at the same time, then barricaded the doors.

For every actual sit-down, hundreds of employers fearful of potential strikes raised their workers' wages, as had S. S. Kresge. Again, the mere threat of a strike produced swift results. "More wage increases have been made effective within the past few days by local stores," reported *Women's Wear Daily* on Tuesday, "in anticipation of projected unionization efforts. . . . There are various rumors cropping up regarding sit-down strikes in other local stores, but none have developed." That same day Anthony A. Henk, secretary of the Detroit Retail Merchants Association, "announced that about 800 clerks in 450 meat shops and groceries would receive immediate wage increases averaging 5 percent."

"Brothers, we've got 'em on the run!" exulted the *Detroit Labor News* that week. But it didn't bode well that the *Labor News* wrote the sisters out of labor's success story so quickly; indeed, by Tuesday the focus of stories about Detroit activism had begun to move away from the Woolworth's strikers. New strikes bumped them off the front page, and soon most papers reduced them to a tiny side reference in a general labor story or dropped them altogether.

The new hotel and restaurant strikes in downtown Detroit, moreover, siphoned off the organizing support of Louis Koenig, Mira Komaroff, Floyd Loew, and other union staffers, who now spent their days helping with other efforts. Mary Davis, a rank-and-file union waitress at the time, remembers going down to pay a solidarity visit at Woolworth's on Monday or Tuesday, as a fellow member of Local 705. The picket line was small, she recalls—maybe thirty people. Five or six of the picketers were left-wing activists like herself, but the rest were very depressed and discouraged Woolworth strikers, all of them women in their twenties or thirties who weren't inside because of family commitments or because they hadn't been at work the day the strike began. They told Mary that the strikers weren't getting very much support from the union, and that they were very worried.

We don't know much about exactly what was going on within the store on Tuesday or the next day, precisely because the press had by and large moved on to other stories. *Life* magazine showed up on one of these days, and while it captured the two women sliding down bannisters in their funny playsuits, other women they spoke to admitted to being bored. We can only wonder if everyone was getting along after all that time in close quarters together. One woman photographed by *Life* had abandoned the three-person mattresses on the floor and made a bed for herself on a countertop. By mid-week the women had exhausted the store's supply of sanitary napkins, and new supplies had to be brought in. At some point during the occupation, one woman miscarried.

Would they really be able to manage all the logistics necessary to hold out as days stretched into weeks? As a rule, the longer a strike, the more likely it is to be lost. Usually it's either a quick victory within hours or a day, or a long, extended, painful exhaustion of resources, spirits, and public interest, chipping away slowly at solidarity and the workers' power. By now, the first flush of excitement over and press attention waning, the Woolworth's strikers would have had plenty of time to think about what would happen if they lost: they'd certainly lose a week's pay, likely lose their jobs, and maybe even be blacklisted by Detroit's other stores and restaurants. The families of the single women might be rock-solid behind them, or they might be increasingly irritated that they weren't around to help wash the dishes or watch their little brothers at night. The husbands of married strikers might be home patching together meals in proud solidarity, or they might be getting impatient, even angry. And those boyfriends—rather than holding their men, some of the strikers might be letting them slip away.

If they lost the strike, moreover, the negative ripple effects would be immense. And despite all that glorious solidarity and the upsurge of new strikes, Woolworth's still hadn't budged. Tuesday came and went. O. L. Gause, the company's regional supervisor in Cleveland, said only that they were "surveying the situation" in Detroit. "That's all there is to it," he snapped curtly.

STEELMAKERS CAPITULATE TO CIO IN BIG AGREEMENT

Wednesday, March 4. Sort of like a good news, bad news routine. Seemingly out of the blue, U.S. Steel, reaching its own conclusions from the General Motors strike, gave in to the CIO's Steel Workers' Organizing Committee and signed a huge national agreement recognizing the union, granting an eight-hour day and a forty-hour week, and raising wages by 10 percent. It was stunning news, a huge and total victory for the CIO. And it bumped the Woolworth story out of the papers altogether.

But that same Wednesday, Woolworth's, in its first concession, granted a wage increase to thirty-five women who worked in the restaurant of one of its Boston stores. Some full-time workers got free meals "for the first time in the store's history." With delicious obsequiousness, Woolworth's managers first told the women of the increases, then begged, "Remember, now, no sit-down strike."

NEGOTIATIONS BEGIN IN STORE STAY-INS

Then, finally, the company began to cave. On Wednesday night, Woolworth's executives met for the first time in negotiations with the Detroit Woolworth's unions. They parleyed again on Thursday, in the office of Frank Bostroff, secretary of the Michigan Restauranteurs' Association, who served as mediator. On the workers' side were Louis Koenig, from the waiters' and waitresses' union, Louis Walters, from the cooks', and Louis Salter, from the retail clerks'. *Women's Wear Daily* reported that the identity of the Woolworth's representatives had "been guarded closely since they came to Detroit," but that "it is understood that they are vice presidents in charge of operation from the New York City office." The men were eventually revealed to be A. F. Weber, superintendent of the Midwest region, and John R. Powers and H. W. Frank, the rumored vice presidents. The choice of representatives is telling on both sides. Woolworth's thought that this strike was important enough to send in big shots from New York, while the women whose action had forced them to do that didn't even get to be present at the discussions negotiating their own strike settlement.

All day, contradictory rumors flew about as to the progress of the negotiations. One report confided that Woolworth's was "known to favor a settlement before the end of the week." Another cited "reliable sources" as saying that the company was "willing to grant practically all of the wage demands of the strikers, but is considering the possible effect on other stores throughout the country before making [a] decision"—that is, they too were worried about the ripple effect, especially, rumor had it, a settlement's effect on the retail clerks' union.

Friday morning, *Women's Wear Daily* reported that "observers who were inclined to the belief that an early settlement would be reached when negotiations started are less optimistic today."

STRIKE AT DIME STORES ENDS WITH BIG WAGE BOOST

All day Friday they talked. Then, at 5:30 P.M. on Friday, March 5, the strike's seventh day, just in time to avert Koenig's Saturday deadline for expanding the strike and to avoid the boycott in New York, Woolworth's and the unions announced they had reached an agreement.

No question, it was an absolute and clear-cut victory for the strikers. They won an entire laundry list of demands, including the laundry. First, the company agreed to a five-cent an hour increase for all female employees—a 20 to 25 percent raise, depending on each woman's previous rate. New employees would start at $14.50 a week for the first six months. Everyone would get time and a half for overtime, after a forty-eight-hour work week. Future workers would be hired through the unions' offices. Uniforms would be furnished and laundered by the company for free. The vacation schedule would stay the same. Notices of union meetings could be posted on bulletin boards in the women's locker room and bathrooms. And, most amazing of all, the women would be paid at 50 percent of their usual rate for the time they were occupying the store (though not, presumably, for twenty-four-hour days). Without ever striking, the cooks (who were all male) also got a wage increase and shorter working hours. Moreover, the agreement covered not just the two stores that had been taken over, but all forty Woolworth's stores in the city.

Woolworth's got almost nothing in return, just a little clause saying union employees couldn't coerce nonunion coworkers. It did its feeble best to look strong. "The increase in salaries granted to employees in the two Woolworth stores which had sit-down strikes is not to be store-wide," its executives insisted. In a classic pitch for containment, they declared that "each district is operated in accordance with conditions prevailing in that particular sector, and all matters of policy are determined by the regional supervisor."

Needless to say, once the strikers heard of the agreement, they were ecstatic. The women from the second store quickly packed up their things and rushed down to the main store. Then all the women "sang and cheered Vita Terrall, the strike leader, until 8:30, the evacuation deadline." In between they posed for photographers on the big main staircase, holding up giant cardboard letters on sticks that spelled out "WE WON." Over a thousand people—friends, family, "curious onlookers"—jammed the sidewalks outside, cheering and clapping. "The women then marched by twos carrying their grips and bedding," waving American flags and singing, reported the *Detroit Free Press,* in a "victory parade" down to the Lindbergh Room at the Barlum Hotel. Along the way more onlookers cheered and applauded. Once they were all in the room, Koenig read the agreement out loud to the strikers and he and Walters and Salter signed it officially. (None of the striking women got to vote to approve the agreement, or to sign it.) Then an array of speakers stepped forth to congratulate them, including Frances Comfort from the schoolteachers' union, who'd addressed the strikers on their very first day, and Larry Davidow, a lawyer for the UAW. It was a great moment.

On Saturday Woolworth's announced a special sale.

STRIKE SENTIMENT RAMPANT;

CHAIN STORE ORGANIZATION FLOURISHES;

BABS RENOUNCES CITIZENSHIP BUT NOT PROFITS

We don't know what the women did next. But we do know that in the aftermath of their victory its ripple effects swept through the nation's stores and restaurants for over a year.

Dana Frank

The first wave engulfed Detroit. Clerks at the twelve-story Crowley-Milner department store downtown sat down, and after three days won a wage raise, the five-day, forty-hour week, and union recognition. Workers at Federated Department Stores won in a few hours. At Lerner's, it took three days, and by the end of the week three shoe stores had joined in too. Those were just the big shops. "I would be in the local union office and a girl would call up suddenly," Mira Komaroff recalled, "saying 'say, is this Myra? [*sic*] Someone told me to call you. I'm Mamie, over in Liggett's Drug Store. We threw out the manager, chased out the customers and closed up the place. We are "sitting in." What should we do *now?*'"

By the middle of March, other Mamies all over the country were sitting down in the wake of the Woolworth's victory. In New York, workers struck five H. L. Green department stores on March 13. Then the retail clerks' union, just as they had hinted the week before, took on Woolworth's. This time the situation got much dicier. On March 17, forty of seventy workers at the store on 34th Street declared a sit-down strike, but in this case the remaining clerks kept working, so the managers soon reopened the store to customers. Undaunted, "throughout the day, at regular intervals, the strikers snake-danced through the store, chanting 'We're on strike.'" When the managers locked the doors at the end of the day, the women stayed in for the night. To sneak in food and bedding, their allies made a human chain to haul it all up through a second-story window. On the second day police evicted the strikers, but they marched right back in again, and this time took up their usual positions behind the counters and just stood there, not speaking or helping customers. Arrests, skirmishes, and picketing multiplied for days, until finally Mayor Fiorello LaGuardia agreed to mediate. The strikers won a six-month contract granting union recognition, wage increases, a grievance system, time and a half for overtime, and vacations with pay—for all twenty-five hundred Woolworth's workers in the city.

These New York strikers were directly inspired by their Detroit sisters. "DETROIT STRIKERS WIN!! . . . WE CAN WIN TOO! JOIN THE UNION," a leaflet passed out before the strike exhorted. May Brooks, a Communist organizer at the time, captured wonderfully in an oral history both the improvisational character of the sit-downs that erupted in New York and the importance of Detroit and other precedents: "So there we were, and we didn't know what we were going to do, once we blew the whistle—you know, what to expect and with no experience—just feeling this was . . . the tactic now, and . . . this could work. And of course, we'd read and heard about other sit-down strikes that were beginning to take place . . . and were tremendous."

The New Yorkers were even quicker than the Detroit women to drag in poor Barbara Hutton. In one clever organizing leaflet distributed before the New York strike, activists told the mythical story of "Little Barbara Button" who worked at the "Millworks" store at "35th and Wiseway." They devised even better slogans— "Barbara Hutton eats good mutton. Woolworth workers they get nuttin'"—and even appealed directly to the heiress herself in a telegram sent during the strike. Alas, Hutton, having recently purchased a set of emeralds for $1.2 million, was off on a sightseeing tour in the Sahara atop a camel and never responded. Allegedly her new husband pocketed the missive when it arrived and she never saw it.

In December, the "Babs vs. Woolworth girls" plot thickened. That fall, the retail clerks' union in New York went on to achieve success after success, organizing five thousand new workers by the year's end. But when the Woolworth's contract expired at the end of October, the company refused to renew it. Smack in the middle of increasing publicity about the situation, on December 15 Barbara Hutton Mdivani Haugwitz-Reventlow sailed into New York harbor and stopped in town just long enough to sign papers renouncing her American citizenship so she could save $400,000 a year in taxes (she had gained Danish citizenship automatically when she married Reventlow). Barbara's public image plummeted to an all-time low.

The press was relentless. "The shopgirls . . . have been contributing their mites toward [Barbara's] income of $2,000,000 a year," charged Scripps-Howard columnist Westbrook Pegler, "without which their own 'princess' might never have aroused the love of her ideal. Now she has betrayed them for all time."

Woolworth's activists played it to the hilt, launching a new strike three days later. Workers and their allies paraded up and down sidewalks all over town wearing sandwich boards: "BABS RENOUNCES CITIZENSHIP BUT NOT PROFITS." "WHILE WE STRIKE FOR HIGHER PAY, BABS TAKES HER MONEY AND RUNS AWAY." Once again, they telegrammed Barbara: "URGE THAT YOU ORDER MANAGEMENT TO CONCEDE A LIVING WAGE TO THOUSANDS NOW EXISTING ON STARVATION WAGES." She never responded, but Woolworth's executives settled the strike after its first day. As of July 1938, *Life* was still haunting Barbara. It ran a photo of her "wearing richly embroidered Oriental beach pajamas," with the admonition, "She should forget counts who spend her money and remember the Woolworth girls who earn it."

These organizing successes in New York and Detroit were only a few examples of a nationwide uprising of store clerks that year. Frances Comfort, the Detroit teacher, had been right: the strikers had indeed been fighting not only for themselves but for thousands like themselves all over the country. "The situation in Detroit has thoroughly aroused the salespeople everywhere," wrote the retail clerks' national magazine in April. "Retail management is finally aroused to a fuller sense of responsibility and realization that employees are people, not merely groups of automatons, to be herded and managed without regard to human rights and ambitions." The next month they put it even better: "Since the action of the Detroit employees in February, Woolworth and other variety store employees in a number of cities are rebelling against the inhibitions of enforced paternalism that these employers have used in the past to keep their employees loyal to the firm instead of loyal to themselves and fellow workers."

Girl Strikers Occupy Chain Store, Win Big

In the third week of March 1937, picketing in East St. Louis produced a single union contract covering workers at Woolworth's, Grant's, Newberry's, and Kresge stores across the entire city, and a brief strike won a union and increases for workers at four chains in Akron, Ohio. In May, workers in St. Louis got a contract covering fifteen hundred workers at thirty-three Woolworth's stores. That summer victories proliferated like glorious poppies across the national landscape, spreading from variety stores to grocery store chains to department stores—in St. Paul, Minnesota; in Centralia, Washington; in Superior, Wisconson. By the year's end Tacoma, San Francisco, and Duluth had joined the list, along with Seattle, where three thousand clerks in twenty-three stores, including Sears, J. C. Penney, Frederick & Nelson's, the Bon Marche, and Lerner's, won not only the forty-hour week but a pay increase "estimated to increase the income of the employees by at least one half-million dollars." Over sixty years later, unions today in department stores all over the country owe their existence in part to the Woolworth strike.

Last but not least, the Woolworth strike lived on in popular culture. *Pins and Needles,* a new Broadway musical, opened in November of 1938 with a catchy tune, "Chain Store Daisy," about the grievances of a Vassar student laboring at a department store. Two years later, Jean Arthur, Charles Coburn, and Robert Cummings starred in the screwball comedy *The Devil and Miss Jones,* which featured a mean department store owner who goes underground as a salesclerk to break a union at his own store, but, when a strike breaks out, ends up converted to the workers' cause.

DAVID TRIUMPHS OVER GOLIATH IN STUNNING UPSET

All this from a hundred and eight very young, entirely ordinary young women who one day in Detroit decided to stage a sit-down. That was the brilliance of it—it wasn't some mythical superheroes who had pulled it off, but regular young women with no experience of striking, let alone of occupying a major chain store twenty-four hours a day for seven long days. They took on one of the biggest corporate powers of their time and won big, inspiring hundreds of thousands of other ordinary salesclerks—and who knows who else—to stand up (or sit down) for their rights, to claim a living wage, to demand an end to corporate paternalism, and to insist they were indeed live and vibrant human beings, not change-making machines. They danced and made up songs and did each others' nails and slid down bannisters precisely because they were alive and knew it and wanted more from life than fifty-four hours a week of subservience in painful shoes. And they taught the arrogant Woolworth's corporation an enormous lesson.

In retrospect, what they did looks simple, almost easy. But they could easily have lost, and they won because they had an enormous array of powers behind them: the example of the General Motors workers, the force of public opinion, neutrality from the mayor and governor, spectacular solidarity from thousands of allies, and, best of all, their own sense of audacity, of fun, and of faith in themselves.

What's the lesson? With enough allies, with enough inspiration, and with enough daring, anything can happen.

EPILOGUE

Louis Koenig, a.k.a. "Smiley," stayed on as secretary-treasurer of Local 705, the Detroit waiters' and waitresses' union. He retired in 1960 at the age of seventy-two and spent the rest of his life at a nursing home in Florida.

Mira Komaroff stayed on at Local 705 too, first as recording secretary and then, after Koenig retired in 1960, inheriting his job as secretary-treasurer. In 1939 she married and changed her name to Myra Wolfgang. She went on to become an international vice president of the Hotel and Restaurant Employees' International Union in 1952 and a pioneer woman leader in the AFL-CIO, fighting for equal pay and the minimum wage, and helping to found CLUW, the Coalition of Labor Union Women, in 1974. She died of a brain tumor in 1976, a month before her sixty-second birthday.

Floyd Loew was purged from the local in 1943, after he refused to cooperate with Koenig and Komaroff/Wolfgang and cross a picket line during a strike at Harper Hospital in Detroit. He remained active as a dissident rank-and-file activist in HERE for the rest of his life, in Florida, Las Vegas, and Los Angeles. He died in the mid-1990s.

Paul Domeney, the Hungarian waiter, and *Mary Davis*, the union waitress, who both visited the picket line during the Woolworth's strike, were purged from Local 705 in the fall of 1938, for advocating rank-and-file participation in contract negotiations, the right of rank-and-filers to vote on ratification of their own contracts, and one unified union of all restaurant workers. Domeney lost his job at the Book-Cadillac Hotel as a result, and was blacklisted from work in the city's hotels and restaurants. In 1940 he founded an independent union of Detroit restaurant workers, Local 1064, affiliated with the CIO, which survives to this day. He retired to Florida in 1999 at the age of ninety. Mary Davis is still thriving as an independent activist for social justice in Detroit.

In April, 1937, Governor Frank Murphy and other officials cracked down on sit-down strikes in Detroit. Throughout the nation, state and local governments moved swiftly to restore private property rights at the point of a gun, ending the sit-down wave. But the *Congress of Industrial Organizations* nonetheless went on to greater and greater victories throughout the late 1930s and the 1940s. By 1948 it represented almost four and a half million workers in industries all over the country. In 1955, the CIO merged with the AFL to form the AFL-CIO.

The *Woolworth Corporation* continued to expand during the 1940s and 1950s. In February of 1960, a new wave of young people launched sit-ins at its stores throughout the South to protest the chain's refusal to serve African Americans at its lunch counters. Protesters joined them to picket Woolworth's stores throughout the country. The chain finally agreed to serve African Americans, and eventually hired them to work in its stores as well.

Although the Woolworth Corporation acquired new subchains such as Foot Locker and Kinney Shoes and grew to 6,700 stores by 1996, the company failed to keep up with new megastores such as Wal-Mart and Costco in the 1980s and 1990s. In 1997 it reorganized itself as the Venator Corporation and closed all its Woolworth's stores throughout the United States. With the exception of two boxes of photographs of the Woolworth Building, all its records are destroyed or lost, and Woolworth's no longer exists.

Barbara Hutton divorced Kurt Haugwitz-Reventlow in 1941 and went on to marry five more times, to Cary Grant, Prince Igor Troubetzkoy, Porfirio Rubirosa, Baron Gottfried Von Cramm, and Prince Raymond Doan Vinh Na Champassak. She died of anorexia in 1979, at the age of sixty-six.

The *Hotel and Restaurant Employees' International Union,* of which Detroit Local 705 was part, became one of the most progressive and dynamic unions in the country, winning organizing drives in the 1980s and 1990s at Yale University, Las Vegas casinos, and hotels throughout downtown Los Angeles. In 2001 it represents 250,000 workers and is known for its commitment to union democracy, interracial solidarity, and worker militance.

The *Detroit Woolworth's workers* lost their union contract when it came up for renewal in October of 1937. As individual women left the store, management deliberately replaced them with anti-union workers, who didn't then fight to keep the union.

The names of the strikers themselves are lost to the historical record, and we don't know what they did with the rest of their lives. Some of them, presumably, Got Their Man and Held Him. Some of them didn't. Some of them did other things altogether.

ROBIN D. G. KELLEY

~~~~~

Without a Song:
New York Musicians Strike Out
against Technology

PRELUDE: "SMOKE GETS IN YOUR EYES"

On the evening of Saturday, October 10, 1936, a near capacity crowd of one thousand packed into the Times Square Theater, a second-run cinema located on West 42nd Street near Broadway. Around 9:30, an explosion erupted from the vicinity of the empty orchestra pit. The sound was incredibly loud but staccato, like a pistol being fired. Some ducked for cover; the curious peeked over their seats to see what the commotion was about. Within seconds, a rumor began to circulate in one section of the theater that a man had just committed suicide. But before the story made its rounds, moviegoers sitting toward the front began coughing and wheezing, their eyes began to tear, and some were overcome with nausea. This was no gunshot; someone had detonated a homemade tear gas bomb. A few panicked and made a mad rush for the exit, leaving behind coats and hats despite the chilly air of the autumn night. Then cooler heads prevailed as ushers prepared the way for an orderly departure. By the time police arrived, the sidewalk was jam-packed with angry, teary-eyed moviegoers demanding a refund or a rain check.

Martin Levine, the theater's general manager, was just as

shocked by the bombing as the audience. While acknowledging past labor troubles, he insisted that he was unaware of any current disputes that might have brought on such an act. Apparently Levine had forgotten about the mass picketing campaign led by Local 802 of the American Federation of Musicians (AFM) against theaters for firing their in-house musicians with the advent of sound pictures. The campaign was exactly one month old on October 10, 1936, and the AFM had been trying to sustain picket lines at most major theaters in Manhattan as well as in Brooklyn and Queens. But there were no pickets at the Times Square Theater that night, and no one—not even the police—suspected the musicians in any case.

They were right. Less than three weeks later, on the evening of October 29, the movie bombers struck again. The culprits turned out to be projectionists affiliated with Local 306 of the Motion Picture Operators Union, whose members had been replaced by the Allied Motion Picture Operators Union—a "company union" controlled by the Independent Theater Owners Association (ITOA). Local 306 had locked horns with ITOA earlier in the decade, and this was not the first time they had turned to sabotage. During the spring and summer of 1934, renegade members had used tear gas and stink bombs in what had been known in the press as "the movie wars."° But the action of October 29 proved far more serious than anything they had done before. Eight theaters were bombed simultaneously—four in the Times Square area, and the remaining four in other parts of Manhattan and in Brooklyn and Queens. Some

---

°The battle between the projectionists and the theater owners really began around 1930, with the elimination of the disc system. The newer Photophone system required less skill and fewer workers. In the past, projectionists had assistants who helped them handle the sound discs and adjust sound levels, and because breakdowns were frequent, an ability to maintain and repair projectors was a requirement. Under the new system breakdowns were less frequent and projectionists no longer had to deal with cue sheets indicating when to change fader settings since sound levels were now uniform. Their primary task, then, was to load and unload the reels. As a result of this rapid deskilling of the job, projectionists were forced to accept a 25 percent pay cut over two years beginning in 1930.

thirteen thousand patrons were forced to evacuate and at least sixty-two received injuries requiring medical attention. This time the bombs were made with soda bottles and thrown under the seats, sending glass shards everywhere. The lacerations caused by flying glass were worse than the noxious fumes that filled the theaters.

The next day police raided the headquarters of Local 306, arresting thirty-two people and seizing books and other material evidence. Altogether, they deployed well over two hundred plainclothes officers in theaters throughout the city and clamped down on any protest activity in their vicinity. Nevertheless, the bombings continued until the middle of November, when Mayor LaGuardia and a special committee intervened, stepping in to negotiate a settlement between the ITOA and Local 306. The final agreement favored the Motion Picture Operators Union, the biggest concession being the dismantling of the ITOA's company union, whose members were to be absorbed into Local 306.

The projectionists' dramatic victory cast a long shadow over the musicians' efforts to "bring back flesh" to the theater. The fact that neither the theater owners nor the police seemed cognizant of the AFM's grievances as a "labor dispute," let alone suspected for a minute that they might have been behind any of the bombings, speaks to the musicians' lack of visibility. Their struggle to return live musicians to movie theaters had been going on for about a decade, and AFM leaders were convinced that audiences wanted the same. As the union's latest campaign began that October, the AFM's main organ, *International Musician,* carried an editorial claiming that "every poll and every straw vote has always favored the retention or return of Flesh as the case may be and yet nothing is ever done about it." A dispirited and hyperbolic rant, to be sure, for the picket lines were easily ignored by a modern world anxious to check out the latest Fred Astaire and Ginger Rogers flick. Besides, the New York musicians did little more than parade, picket, and propagandize to bring attention to their struggle. In the age of sit-down strikes and sabotage, Local 802 never promoted civil disobedience;

there were no clarinetists taking over projection booths, or trombonists emptying spit valves over huge vats of popcorn, or whole ensembles blocking the screen with renditions of "Nice Work If You Can Get It." And there were no significant acts of solidarity between the AFM and any other unions besides actors' and stagehands' organizations.

But there is a story here, an incredibly important one at that. Embedded in this unremarkable campaign is the tale of what happens when working-class consumption of popular culture overrides the interests or concerns of popular culture workers, in this case, theater musicians. We might go one step further and say it's a story about the limits of solidarity—limits set by employees who are not seen or do not see themselves as "workers," and by working-class consumers whose own self-interest may actually clash with the demands of laboring artists. Finally, and most fundamentally, this is a story about technology and workers' control, and how utterly ill-equipped the union was to deal with the transformation of the *work* of art in the age of mechanical reproduction. Through the AFM "strike" of theaters in 1936, we will better understand the collision between technology and art, work and play, past and future. Grab your popcorn, make yourself comfortable, and leave your blue-collar visions at the theater door.

"PLAYING IN THE DARK"

Musicians are rarely thought of as workers. Instead, we tend to see them as entertainers and, more often than not, powerful celebrities rather than wage laborers. Or we tend to think of musicians as engaged in "play" rather than work. And yet, if we think about the work of making music and the context in which this work takes place, we cannot help but acknowledge the myriad ways musicians are affected by the whims and caprices of capital, the routinization of labor, and the often dehumanizing conditions of production. On the other hand, musicians are not just another group of skilled wage laborers. They straddle class lines and historically possess a kind of cultural authority that may belie their material class position.

Throughout the nineteenth century, most Western musicians thought of themselves as an elite group of artists, and they embraced a hierarchy of musical culture that distinguished "refined" music from folk or vernacular idioms. Furthermore, musicians are not considered workers because they do not work, they *perform*. They produce art, and as such, their work is often also a conscious act of self-expression. In some instances, their self-expression may come into conflict with the goals of their employers. As creative laboring artists, they could be fired not only for incompetence but also for innovation. Indeed, one of the central roles of a musicians' union is to arbitrate such disputes between musicians and employers (bandleaders, club owners, etc.).

By the turn of the century the situation had changed slightly. The increasing commercialization of music and the changing and expanding market generated new opportunities for folk and "popular" musicians. The National League of Musicians (NLM) had been the dominant protective organization in the late nineteenth century, and its president, Owen Miller, understood that new employment opportunities in the industrial age required a new type of bargaining unit. He sought to make the NLM more like a trade union and to affiliate with the American Federation of Labor, but many members resisted, causing Miller and his more labor-oriented colleagues to form the American Federation of Musicians in 1900.

The AFM's first president and undisputed leader was a thirty-seven-year-old clarinetist named Joseph Weber. Born in a small village in the old Austro-Hungarian empire, Weber had immigrated to New York with his family at the age of fourteen. He learned music from his father, who worked on and off as a musician, and by his late teens he was playing professionally in a touring band. In 1891, he married violinist Gisela Liebholdt and continued to perform throughout the western United States. He also joined the NLM, serving as vice president of the Seattle local and a principal organizer for Local 26 in Denver. In 1895, he moved to Cincinnati, where he took up the presidency of Local 3 of the Musicians Protective Union. After achieving the presidency of the AFM, Weber held on to the post for forty years. Part of his popularity stemmed from his recognition that musicians were, indeed, workers and needed to defend themselves against exploitation. "We musicians are employed under the same conditions of any other workers," Weber explained. "We may be artists, but we still work for wages.... [We] are exploited by our employers in the same manner as any other wage-earners who stand alone. Therefore we must organize, cooperate and become active in the economic field like other workers."

The AFM was founded during a time of increased employment opportunities for musicians, partly the result of the emergence of cinema. By 1910, some ten thousand theaters across the nation showed silent films as their core entertainment, and they all required musicians to provide a "soundtrack" and to perform between reels. The proliferation of movie houses generated a ten-fold increase in the number of musicians employed in theaters. By 1926, about twenty-two thousand musicians were working in theater pits across the country, comprising about one-fifth of the total membership of the AFM. Two years later, New York City theaters alone employed over three thousand musicians.

In the early days of silent cinema, theatergoers were treated to what amounted to a two-hour variety show: newsreels, vaudeville acts (including blackface minstrel performances), and a feature film. (In some cases in order to fit all the performances into the time allotted, projectionists might speed up a film.) What musicians played to accompany films varied, as did the size of the band—which could range from a fifteen-piece orchestra to a single organist. The bigger houses maintained a library of sheet music to draw on, and sometimes debates arose between bandleaders and theater owners over what was appropriate. The failure or success of musical accompaniment became a major issue in the trade magazines. As one theater owner advised in *Moving Picture World* (October 30, 1909), "Get a good piano player, who can read any music at sight and make him or her attend strictly to business. . . . Often and often have I entered a theater while the film was running and seen the piano player industriously engaged in talking to a friend, dividing her attention impartially between the friend and a wad of gum."

Of greater concern was whether or not the music seemed appropriate to the action on the screen. Some African American bands were notorious for subverting a film by engaging in playful musical signifying that would have horrified studio executives. Black columnist Dave Peyton, critic for the *Chicago Defender,* attacked these moments of musical levity as unbecoming of the race. Speaking of his experiences in black theaters, he observed, "During a death scene . . . you are likely to hear the orchestra jazzing away on 'Clap Hands, Here Comes Charlie.' . . . There is entirely too much 'hokum' played in our Race picture houses. It only appeals to a certain riff-raff element who loudly clap hands when the orchestra stops, misleading the leader to believe that his efforts are winning the approval of the entire audience."

Of course, black theater musicians had no monopoly on "hokum," but they did tend to play a more important role in the overall makeup of a show. In some cases, audiences were drawn to the theater more for the band than for the movie itself. In Harlem during the teens, theatergoers lined up outside the Lafayette to hear Hallie Anderson's all-female band, or they might catch her at Harlem's Douglas Theater, where she was the house organist. Fats Waller was legendary for his film accompaniments. Fellow pianist Mary Lou Williams remembers how the audience responded: "He was just a sensation in New York, when they'd turn the light on people would scream, when he sat down, people would scream: I never saw such a thing. When he finished, that was the end; they had to let it cool off."

Given these kinds of subversions, is it any wonder that studios and theaters attempted to standardize musical accompaniment? Some movie houses turned to piano rolls, and in 1910 Wurlitzer and

J. P. Seeburg introduced special "automatic" keyboards to accompany films, called photoplayers. They contained several rolls of music and could play thirty or more songs without repetition—each chosen to represent a different emotion. An assortment of bells and horns could be activated for special effect by pulling straps or depressing pedals.

Since few theaters could afford photoplayers, however, and most needed bands to perform vaudeville numbers, the studios sought to control musical accompaniment for films in another way, by providing cue sheets. Cue sheets were musical fragments with precise time frames and sound effects "cued" to the titles and action on the screen. Usually prepared by a music editor and distributed with the film itself, these were not intended to be full musical scores, but they did provide musical direction. The need for some standard of accompaniment sparked a cottage industry of guides and collections of cue sheets, beginning with Gregg A. Frelinger, *Motion Picture Piano Music: Descriptive Music to Fit the Action, Character or Scene of Moving Pictures* (1909), which contained fifty-one short pieces with functional titles meant to correspond with stock characters or events on screen. Edith Lang and George West's *Musical Accompaniment of Moving Pictures: A Practical Manual for Pianists and Organists* (1920) provided more specific guidelines for musicians, including explicit ideas about how to convey race, ethnicity, and nature. To support an exotic scene from "the Orient," for instance, one must play Oriental music. "As a rule," they advise, "Oriental music is distinguished rather by a peculiar inflection of the melody than by variety of harmonic treatment. The latter belongs to the Occident. Therefore it will often suffice if the player adheres for his accompaniment to a droning bass or either an open fifth or fourth or a stereotyped rhythmical figure that is indicative of either the languor of the scene (opium dens, harems, etc.) or of its typical movement (Arabian caravans, Oriental dancers, Chinese junks). A few works may be suggested here, as offering a great deal of useful material of distinctly Oriental color, such as 'Scheherazade' by

Rimsky-Korsakov ... the opera 'Lakme' by Delibes and the ballet 'Namouna' by Lalo ... the opera 'Madame Butterfly' by Puccini, the piano suites 'Dreamer's Tales' and 'Betel, Jade and Ivory' by Peterkin." All of the works selected are by Western composers who imagine "the Orient." The same holds true in their advice for accompanying what they identified as "Southern scenes (negro activities, etc.)," for they suggested turning to the songs of Stephen Foster in order to capture the authentic Negro sensibility.

"HOW DO YOU KEEP THE MUSIC PLAYING?"

By the late 1920s, the emergence of sound film technology rendered cue sheets and these sorts of manuals obsolete. Now filmmakers and music editors could put their Orientalist fantasies directly onto a soundtrack without having to worry about the capabilities or dispositions of local musicians. Briefly, Warner Brothers introduced the first successful sound system, called Vitaphone, which employed a separate disc synchronized to the film. A year later, Fox Films introduced Movietone, an improved version of the Vitaphone system. The disc system proved unsatisfactory, however, because the discs were bulky and broke easily, they contained varying levels of surface noise, and they were only good for about twenty showings. Besides, given the nature of national distribution, theater owners occasionally received the wrong disc. Most of these problems were solved, however, when Western Electric introduced the Kinegraphone, better known as the Photophone. By placing the recording track directly onto the film itself, the Photophone system improved sound quality, eliminated most problems of synchronization, eased editing, and significantly reduced the level of skill required of projectionists.

When Paramount, MGM, and United Artists decided to adopt Photophone in 1929, many local theaters across the country were forced to change their projection system or risk going out of business (although there were still Vitaphone and Movietone holdouts well into the 1930s). And in some cases, the big studios moved in to purchase local theaters to add to their chains. While monopoly and rapid technological change led to the loss of jobs throughout the movie industry—all of this synchronized to the stock market crash and the onset of the Great Depression—the studios did not appear to be losing profits. Al Jolson's *The Jazz Singer* (1927)—technically the second full-length sound film, following *Don Juan*, which premiered a year earlier—broke all box office records, and Jolson's next film, *The Singing Fool*, did even better. The number of theaters equipped for sound rose from 157 in 1927 to 13,880 in 1931—representing nearly two-thirds of all theaters in the country.

Evidently, theatergoers did not miss "flesh": attendance increased dramatically, from an average of fifty million a week in 1926 to ninety million a week in 1930. The elimination of live musicians also meant the disappearance of vaudeville, enabling owners to reduce admission prices to as little as twenty-five to fifty cents for double and triple features. And now that the owners no longer had to abide by union regulations regarding musicians' hours, they could show films all day long. Ironically, the Depression conditions enhanced theater profits as a growing army of jobless people escaped the cold, the heat, or their general frustrations by spending their afternoons at the movies. A random survey revealed that on one day in 1932 a Washington Heights theater took in $225 in the afternoon and only $37 in the evening.

Although the new technology was expensive, costing anywhere between $9,000 and $15,000 for a medium to large movie house, theater owners easily made up for the expense by firing their live musicians. Maintaining a fifteen-piece orchestra, for example, could run to almost $50,000 per year. Beyond saving theater owners the cost of a band, the transition to sound rationalized film operations, eliminating problems caused by disputes over song selections, no-shows, or uneven performances, not to mention out-of-tune pianos or defective organ pipes. Furthermore, recorded soundtracks do not go out on strike or demand higher wages. Making film music still required musicians' labor, but production shifted

from the site of performance to the studio, where Taylorist principles of rational production were the order of the day.° The studios
erected a sharp division of labor that included a range of full-time
and part-time musicians, arrangers, composers, copyists, and music
librarians. Indeed, the music library of a single studio claimed the
third largest collection of music of any library in the United States,
with holdings of well over eighty thousand compositions. Music
production resembled an assembly line: film composers rarely
oversaw orchestrations or arrangements, and in some cases a primary composer might turn over his/her basic melodic lines to another composer to be harmonized. While this generated more work
for composers, it stripped them of any control over their work. Studios owned and controlled everything, and at this point composers
were among the few music workers not unionized.

As production changed, so did the product. According to Leonid
Sabaneev's *Music for the Films,* one of the first "handbooks" for
composers and conductors, sound film required "strict and solid
composition" as opposed to the "mere improvisation" characteristic
of the silents, partly in order to coordinate music with speech and
various naturalistic noises. Music for mass production, therefore,
meant mass-produced music. The film composer, Sabaneev warns,
"is hardly ever asked to create anything new, anything of his
own. . . . Little value is attached to a talent for novelty or invention;
in fact it is considered superfluous, and a hindrance rather than otherwise. The level of intelligence of the vast cinema audience is, on
the average, low, and therefore it is useless to astonish it with har-

°Taylorism, or "scientific management," is a method of organizing production by
separating manual from mental labor and eliminating what is deemed "unnecessary" motion in order to enhance efficiency. The result is the routinization and deskilling of work. Pioneered by Frederick Winslow Taylor, the basic principle behind
Taylorism is to divide the labor of building/manufacturing a product into separate,
simple tasks that could be executed by unskilled labor. The creative and intellectual
work of design and conception would be placed in the hands of management. Simi-
larly, in the field of film music the creative work of choosing or inventing appropriate music is taken out of the hands of the musicians, who are now either playing selected scores in the theater or recording in studios.

monic subtleties, with cunning devices of a purely musical type, which only a musician could appreciate." So it should come as no surprise that authority over the recording/performance of the music rested not with the bandleaders or musicians themselves but with program directors and producers. Very few were musicians, and yet they often selected music, determined length, dynamics, position and volume of microphones, general sound levels, and instrumentation. The program director gave signals to musicians from inside the control booth—the embodiment of the fact that control had shifted from the workers in the orchestra pits or on stage to engineering booths owned and operated by the big studios.

There were hidden racial and gender dimensions, as well, to the restructuring and rationalizing of film music. While men had certainly dominated the world of instrumental music in general, there had been quite a few women pianists and organists working in theaters before the transition to "talkies." The sound revolution eliminated virtually all women from the field, in part because studio work was limited to a small group of elite instrumentalists. Moreover, film music's center of creative gravity shifted from the improvising musician to the composer and the musical director—positions women simply did not occupy. Likewise, very few African American musicians could obtain studio work in Hollywood before the 1950s, aside from occasional novelty films featuring figures such as Duke Ellington or Count Basie. When theaters in black communities transitioned to sound, it meant replacing black musicians with lily-white studio orchestras whose tightly controlled scores were not supposed to draw audience attention. One can only imagine how profoundly the movie-going experience must have changed in black theaters.

The inequities of race and gender, however, were overshadowed by the fact that the vast majority of theater musicians lost their jobs with the transition to sound. Only a relative handful of musicians were able to secure studio work, and nearly all of them were concentrated in Southern California. In 1930, there were about 14,000 musicians employed in theaters nationwide, already down from 26,000 less than four years earlier. By 1934, the number of theater musicians had dropped to a paltry 4,100, and the American Federation of Musicians faced its worst crisis since its inception four decades earlier.

"THEY CAN'T TAKE THAT AWAY FROM ME"

The first signs of displacement by theater owners generated sharp resistance from musicians. As early as 1927, musicians employed by Skouras's Grand Central Theater in St. Louis successfully fought management's plan to lay off its orchestra during a run of Vitaphone films. Astonishingly, the AFM local negotiated a settlement whereby the musicians received seven weeks of full salaries for idle time. The following year, the union picketed the Idlewild Theater in East St. Louis—also owned by the Skouras brothers—for letting its orchestra go. Trade unionists throughout the city supported the musicians by refusing to cross the picket line. When the strike was finally settled, the Skouras brothers agreed to stop laying off orchestras wholesale, and the Grand Central kept on seven musicians who played two or three minutes between films but were paid at full scale. At other theaters, musicians were hired to play only about ninety seconds during each show but paid a weekly salary. These arrangements were short-lived, however; within two years most St. Louis theater musicians were unemployed.

Throughout the summer and fall of 1928, AFM locals across the country followed the St. Louis example and tried to fight back. With strikes erupting in Des Moines, Omaha, Seattle, Chicago, and elsewhere in a failed attempt to halt the layoffs, it is not surprising that the impact of talkies became the main topic of the AFM's 1928 national convention, held in Louisville, Kentucky. Some delegates suggested that theaters raise admission prices in order to continue paying musicians, others proposed accepting lower wages, and a few supported the radical though problematic demand that the union ban members from studio recording (which would have denied struggling musicians access to hundreds of new jobs). The prevailing strategy came from AFM president Joseph Weber, and it was *not* based on the union principles of worker solidarity. Instead, he proposed a heavily financed public relations campaign to convince audiences of the superiority of live over "canned" music. While he was all for scientific progress, he argued that "art can not be mechanized" and that recorded music "can not approach the genuine article. Music is dependent for its quality upon the mood of the artist. The public will not be allowed to realize this." In other words, musicians are not simply craftsmen who control their labor, and it is their mood, their personality, the very act of creating that makes their vocation special and unique.

Weber paid for the campaign by levying a 2 percent tax on AFM members, the proceeds of which went directly to a "Theater Defense Fund" that soon evolved into the Music Defense League. By the end of 1928, the first year of the campaign, the union had collected about $1.5 million for the fund. The money was initially used to take out advertisements in newspapers, magazines, and on billboards. Most were dramatic, like an ad with "Sick Houses" emblazoned across the top, implying that theaters were doing poorly owing to the lack of live music. In "troublous times," the ad stated, men and women want *"living music*—cheery and glamorous atmosphere, a place to forget cares for the moment," and, "the all-sound house does not fit the bill. However worthy its screen shows may be, such a theatre remains a dark and cheerless spot—likely to become a sick house." For all of Weber's protestations that he was not a Luddite, a few of the ads seemed to directly attack technology. One read, "Is His Substitution for Real Music a Success?" over a picture of an iron man ripping out the strings of a harp while a dog howls and an angel cries. In 1931, the AFM extended its publicity campaign to include "Living Music Day." Sponsored by union locals and local businesses, participants held outdoor or free concerts, "block dancing in the streets," and parades, all to demonstrate live performance's "superiority over Canned Music."

In March of 1929, Weber met with the members of Local 802 in New York City to discuss his publicity campaign, but local leaders and rank-and-file members had other ideas. One particular group, under the auspices of the Musical Mutual Protective Union, planned a mass march against joblessness and technological displacement, but they were unable to secure a parade permit. Feeling the brunt of the crisis, members J. M. Camuti and Charles Palizzolo proposed a set of recommendations that might save jobs and reduce unemployment. Among other things, they wanted the union to stipulate that orchestras that put in a minimum amount of time not be fired until the end of the season, and they proposed a sharing of work by reducing the work week to five days, shortening the workday, and distributing jobs more evenly. "The work [ought] to be controlled by the Union and divided equally and not with favoritism." Specifically, they called for rules against union members having more than one job, doubling on more than one instrument, and working on Movietone or Vitaphone productions for more than three hours per day. If a company needed more than three hours of work, they would have to hire another orchestra.

A committee of ten was formed to develop these ideas and by May they produced a comprehensive resolution calling for the negotiation of new wage scales with the Theater Managers Association, rules regarding the minimum number of musicians theaters must keep employed, and a four-week clause stipulating that bands providing satisfactory work for that amount of time could not be fired until the season ended. They also demanded that the price of "canned music" in any of its manifestations be increased by 25 percent, the proceeds to go to a local relief fund for musicians, and insisted on collecting royalties "for every synchronized picture in all theatres," monies that would also go to the relief fund. Finally, in an effort to get a handle on competition from musicians migrating to New York City, the resolution raised Local 802's initiation fee to $100 and limited new members to twenty per month. And, of course, the local promised to support the publicity efforts of the Music Defense League.

Local 802 was not able to enforce any of the demands they made on the theater owners, and conditions only got worse with the deepening of the Depression nationwide. Even the film industry suffered major financial losses: Warner Brothers reportedly lost some $8 million in 1931, then $14 million the following year. According to Paramount's executives, their losses compelled them to lay off five thousand employees. In response, the AFM's national leadership proposed a staggered system of employment in those theaters that still used musicians, whereby unemployed musicians would replace those with jobs one out of four weeks. Weber saw this as a way of sharing jobs without wage reductions or costs to the theater. The plan could be carried out at the employers' discretion so long as an equal number of musicians could work for at least one week out of four; the musician holding the regular gig could not then take someone else's job for a week as part of the staggering system since this would defeat the whole purpose of the plan.

Within Local 802, a huge debate erupted over the "spread-the-work" campaign, drawing opposition from both leaders and the rank and file. Local vice president William Feinberg submitted a report critical of the plan, arguing that assigning one job to two or three people amounted to "a coolie wage for all." It never really worked in New York, although there were various proposals for modified spread-the-work plans, including one in which the employer would pay a 50 percent "standby" fee to the union for musicians deemed indispensable. In other words, the musicians in demand would be paid 50 percent above scale, the difference to be paid to the union. The intended effect would be more work for other musicians, if an employer did not want to pay the additional fee, and/or more money for the union's relief efforts. An interesting idea to be sure, for it implies that the employers, not the musicians, should bear the responsibility for ameliorating the hardship caused by the decline in the number of available jobs.

Supporters of the plan argued that some musicians profited over others not only by their personal connections but by their association with certain bands, certain record labels, and certain types of music (i.e., symphonies vs. jazz). The result, they complained, was inequality—and some union members had two jobs while others "of equal competence are entirely unemployed." But there were problems in defining competence and assessing differing skill levels between musicians. Indeed, the biggest complaint about the spread-the-work campaign was that it resulted in uneven bands and orchestras. Besides, it never solved the immediate problem: musicians needed more work.

Since Local 802 could not create more jobs, its leaders focused their energies on providing relief for its members. Beginning in 1934, the year America was hit with a massive nationwide wave of strikes in over a dozen industries, the year when Depression-era class warfare had probably reached its peak, Local 802 approached New York's bourgeoisie with hat in hand. The city's elite, many of whom owned or invested in those industries being struck, were more than happy to do their part for musicians, for they found it simply appalling that so many "worthy artists" had to struggle like ordinary blue-collar laborers.

Under the leadership of Dr. Walter Damrosch and the extraordinarily wealthy philanthropist/patron of the arts Mrs. Vincent Astor, a Musicians' Emergency Fund was created to raise $400,000 for relief. At the time, Damrosch was one of the most prominent and visible men in the world of music. A German emigré who had lived in the United States since 1871, Damrosch had the distinction of conducting the Metropolitan Opera, the New York Philharmonic Society, and the Symphony Society, and of having composed major choral works and operas, including *The Scarlet Letter* and *The Man Without a Country*. Especially noteworthy, however, is his check-

ered history with musicians' unions. Just one year after his brother
Frank, a prominent left-wing conductor and teacher, founded the
working-class-based People's Choral Union in 1892, Walter Damrosch was fined by the NLM for hiring Danish cellist Anton Hegner
for the New York Symphony Society without first advertising for
and auditioning American musicians. The NLM had established
strict rules against "importing" musicians from outside the country.
To protest Hegner's hiring, the entire orchestra refused to play,
generating what was probably the first strike by an American orchestra. In 1905, Damrosch was fined again for a similar violation,
this time by the AFM. Moreover, in 1927, while the AFM locked
horns with the big radio networks, he had accepted an appointment
as musical adviser to NBC. Nevertheless, in the end Damrosch
sympathized with struggling musicians even if he wasn't the most
union-oriented person.

The money raised by the Musicians' Emergency Fund assisted
about four thousand musicians by defraying medical costs, staving
off evictions, helping with groceries, and protecting artists from
having to sell off their instruments. Mayor LaGuardia enthusiasti-
cally supported the campaign, declaring the week of December 10
through 17 "Musicians' Week." The highlights of the campaign included a fundraising auction held at Jascha Heifetz's penthouse
apartment at 247 Park Avenue. Like Damrosch, the Russian-born
Heifetz was a huge celebrity in the music world, developing a reputation as one of the greatest violinists in the world. Selling off items
ranging from a miniature silver violin to a pair of jeweled cufflinks,
the auction brought in a grand total of $4,366.°

Meanwhile, as Local 802 sought to build public support for live
music and helped the city's elite do its charity work for the arts, the
very theaters that had laid off musicians began to blow up—literally.
Recall that 1934 was also the year that renegade members of Local

---

°The relief campaign continued the following year, but in 1935 the union also
turned to the WPA for assistance. However, because WPA projects paid below
standard union wages, Local 802 spent a good deal of time picketing their offices.

306 of the Motion Picture Operators Union began planting stink bombs in theaters that had locked their members out. Interestingly, union records are virtually silent on the bombings and the local's leaders were never called upon to make a statement. Nevertheless, the wave of police repression that came down on the operators' union probably had a chilling effect on any talk within the AFM of militant action directed at theaters. In fact, the bombings prompted the city to temporarily ban mass picketing in front of theaters. Anyone barring the entrance or exit of a theater could be arrested. But it was not enough to put a stop to the bombings. Indeed, as we have seen already, the militant bombers of operators' Local 306 would provide the background noise for the musicians' strike against the theaters in 1936—for better or for worse.

INTERLUDE: "UNTIL THE REAL THING COMES ALONG"

Patience, dear reader. I know you are anxious to get to the *strike,* but in our story the context is everything. The strike itself represents a confused response to a series of transformations extending far beyond the employment of musicians. At the heart of the problem is what critic/philosopher Walter Benjamin identified as the way a work of art—and here he is primarily speaking of the impact of photography on the visual arts—changes in the "age of mechanical reproduction." Benjamin's interrogation is central to the entire history of music under capitalism, for efforts to "rationalize" and perfect music making in a market-driven world have led to inventions intended to eliminate human error or to capture flawless performances for posterity as well as for mass production and distribution.

In the 1850s, steam calliopes were introduced to replace brass bands on Mississippi river boats. Around the turn of the century the player piano came into being, and then the jukebox, followed by the radio. With the onset of the Great Depression, musicians and even some composers were genuinely alarmed about their future, as radio stations increasingly replaced live orchestras with recorded music and jukeboxes appeared more frequently in restaurants and clubs. And if that wasn't bad enough, in 1934 a subsidiary of the North American Company, the Muzak Corporation, introduced a system to wire music directly into hotels and restaurants, and later into retail stores. Muzak made it possible for one band to play simultaneously for many venues.

The American Society of Composers, Authors, and Publishers (ASCAP) officially sounded the alarm in a small book titled *Nothing Can Replace Music*. Published in 1933, it contained essays attacking the use of recording technology and radio, including one titled "Mechanization Presents Serious Danger to Musical Art." Yet not everyone in the music world agreed. In fact, it's a bit ironic that the musicians' struggle to survive a brave new world of recording technology occurred during an era of heightened musical populism.

As evidenced by the resurgence of American folk music, this was an age when radical composers like Marc Blitzstein, Charles Ives, Aaron Copland, Earl Robinson, and Bernard Herrmann ruled the American scene with an expressed commitment to reach a broader audience. Many of them viewed the radio as one of their primary venues for reaching the masses. Works such as Marc Blitzstein's "I've Got the Tune" and Earl Robinson's "Ballad for Americans" were prepared specifically for radio broadcast. Seeing the technologies of mass production as a benefit rather than a hindrance, some composers also found the same radical potential in cinema. Indeed, Aaron Copland relished the fact that the Depression generated a need for "functional music," which for him had exciting possibilities that could be realized in cinema:

> In all the arts the Depression had aroused a wave of sympathy for and identification with the plight of the common man. In music this was combined with the heady wine of suddenly feeling ourselves—the composers, that is—needed as never before. Previously our works had been largely self-engendered: no one asked for them: we simply wrote them out of our own need. Now, suddenly, functional music was in de-

mand as never before. Motion-picture and ballet companies, radio stations and schools, film and theater producers discovered us. The music appropriate for the different kinds of cooperative ventures undertaken by these people had to be simpler and more direct. (Quoted in Flinn, *Strains of Utopia*)

The celebration of American folk music as an embodiment of older pastoral values clashed with the problem of making music in the age of mechanical reproduction—the very source of the musicians' struggle. Interestingly enough, this contradiction was almost never remarked upon by union leaders. Even in the pages of the *International Musician* (organ of the AFM), alongside a stirring account of Local 802's protest against the demise of theater work, conductor Leopold Stokowski of the world-renowned Philadelphia Orchestra defended film as a means to spread art music to the masses. "It seems to us high time," he wrote, "that we begin to help realize the great possibilities of the present-day sound film for multiplying the audience for the world's richest and most satisfying music." (He did more than write for film; he made occasional appearances, most notably in Disney's 1940 production *Fantasia.*) Responding to the fear that in swing-crazed America jazz might replace serious concert music, he believed that mechanical reproduction—especially film—was a way to bring serious music back to the public without having to compete with "low" art. "Bach," he wrote, "has certainly nothing to fear from the hottest jazz arrangement.... The color and glitter of instrumentation which dance bands have come to use lately can be traced to the rich storehouse of effects in the best classical music."

Stokowski's observation raises yet another submerged issue in the struggle against mechanical reproduction: the fear of too much populism, especially populism of the Negro variety. As one St. Louis musician complained, radio and "mechanical playing" had changed tastes and thus made it difficult for "serious" musicians to find work. "Many of the finer artists," he added, "have refused even to be starved into playing jazz." He then wondered if "public taste ever will get back to its former standards." In other words, he partly blamed the unemployment situation on the dominance of jazz and the lowbrow tastes of audiences.

This complaint might be exaggerated, but it does hit upon a sore spot in the political economy of Depression-era art. As musician/scholar George Lewis once said, T. W. Adorno and the Frankfurt School hated jazz because they feared their competitors: jazz was threatening to become *the* art music of the twentieth century. And I would add that these fears were not simply a matter of collapsing class hierarchies alone. Musicians labor in different genres, each one carrying specific class, race, and gender implications, which reproduce a cultural hierarchy that determines conditions of work and pay. In music these differentials are not based on skill level but on a racialized, gendered, and class-based "high/low" cultural divide. A glance at Local 802's 1936 wage scale makes the point. Whereas musicians in dance bands received a minimum of $42 for a seven-day work week consisting of five-hour evenings and three matinees (a total of forty-four hours), concert performers earned $60 for six evenings of four-hour performances, or twenty-four hours of work per week. And they were entitled to an additional $10 for Sunday evening concerts. Not surprisingly, film studio musicians fetched the highest rates, earning $200 for a five-and-a-half-day work week not to exceed thirty-three hours.

While many musicians were capable of crossing these genre boundaries—and did so regularly—the work cultures remained fairly discrete. Artists in "high" genres tended to denigrate popular music and the artists who created it—particularly black music. The policing of these boundaries grows out of a long tradition of marginalizing what is in fact central to American culture: blackness. It is not an accident that the first successful talkie was a performance of blackness, Al Jolson's *The Jazz Singer.* Nor can we forget that the first "hit song" of the sheet music age was T. D. Rice's "Jim Crow Song," or that the first literary best-seller was Harriet Beecher Stowe's *Uncle Tom's Cabin.* More to the point, immediately after the success of Jolson's blackface performance, the studios rushed out to sign up black acts for sound film.

Convinced that song and dance could most effectively show off the new technology, the big studios produced several films featuring African American musical entertainers. In 1929, Paramount released several such films, including *Music Hath Charms, The Framing of the Shrew,* and *Melancholy Dame,* a short "plantation" musical based on a story by white Southerner Octavus Roy Cohen. That same year RKO released *Black and Tan,* featuring Duke Ellington, *St. Louis Blues,* starring the great blues singer Bessie Smith, and the classic all-black musical *Hallelujah!* Black musical performance also functioned as a replacement for certain kinds of vaudeville acts performed in theaters before the advent of talkies. *On with the Show,* which also appeared in 1929, opens with eager fans anxious to hear Ethel Waters sing "Am I Blue." And the ad for *Hearts of Dixie* read like a vaudeville/minstrel playbill, promising "Negro spirituals . . . sung by a magnificent chorus—stevedores and roust-abouts croon thrilling melodies as the 'Nellie Bly' pulls into [the] wharf—cake walks, folk dances, native jazz orchestras, the birth of the blues . . . [all] in a breathlessly beautiful and realistic panorama of life along the levees and in the cotton fields with a cast of 200 *Native Entertainers.*"

The wave of black musical films turned out to be short-lived, but the prominence of jazz in popular culture continued. Complexions changed, however, as the kings of the "swing era" turned out to be white bandleaders like Benny Goodman, Tommy Dorsey, Glenn Miller, and Paul Whiteman, and their work found some acceptance in the hallowed concert halls of high culture. Although purists balked at the practice, the leading swing bands "jazzed" the classics, transforming songs such as Debussy's "Reverie" and Ravel's "Pavane" into swing numbers. Thus the shift in film music production from local musicians to all-white studio orchestras coincided with the "Whitemanning" of the jazz age.

By the late 1930s, swing had become the music of Middle America. AFM president Joseph Weber even devoted a lengthy column in the *International Musician* to the evolution of swing as an important musical development. What did not happen, however, was the incorporation of swing into film music *per se,* that is, into the scores or the soundtracks that accompanied the action on the screen. Although swing bands were employed fairly frequently in 1930s cinema in front of the camera in cameo shots or as background for dance scenes, as historian Caryl Flinn points out, film scores in the 1930s—the era of mass production—were more likely to embody the utopian strains of nineteenth-century romanticism than the modernism that marked the first half of the twentieth century.

So that poor St. Louis musician need not have worried too much, for black music without black bodies had become "serious" music, though still quite inferior to *real* concert music. All he'd have to do now was learn the changes.

"STRIKE UP THE BAND"

By the summer of 1936, the AFM's public relations campaign had failed miserably to sway popular opinion. Audiences embraced sound film and often found the quality of music to be higher than what live orchestras had produced a decade earlier—that is, if they could remember the day of the old silents at all. Realizing that nothing would change without militant action, Local 802 leaders decided that a more confrontational strategy was needed to persuade the theaters to bring back live music and vaudeville acts. After spending much of August planning and debating, the union held a mass meeting on September 10 to inaugurate a campaign to bring "flesh" back to the motion picture theaters. Close to five thousand musicians, actors and "friends of stage shows" showed up at the Manhattan Opera House to hear speeches by union leaders and supporters, including the "father of the blues," W. C. Handy, and Rose Schneiderman, the popular secretary of the Women's Trade Union League.

Schneiderman opened with the comment that she had never addressed "a meeting of artists," but she was nonetheless in sympathy with the plight of theater musicians and promised the support of the city's working women in order to ensure their success. Her remark was telling, for it unwittingly revealed the ambivalence of organized labor to the "laboring artist" and thus exposed one of the limits to solidarity. But Local 802 secretary Fred Birnbach apparently thought that organized labor could deliver the collective strength that the musicians would need to succeed. He called for the cooperation of the entire labor movement in making the demand for living entertainment and proposed a boycott of neighborhood theaters if they completely shifted to recorded sound. The rally ended with the passing of a resolution pledging not to patronize theaters that did not employ musicians. Underlying the resolution, however, was a presumption carried over from the local union's failed publicity campaign, one that accepted as a given that live music was a natural "workers" demand. The resolution asserted that musicians had been "thrown out of theaters in complete disregard for the public's love for live entertainment," as well as disregard for the economic consequences for musicians and actors themselves.

Over the next few weeks, the union picketed theaters throughout the city, organized a parade through Harlem to bring attention to the campaign, printed up fifty thousand buttons, and distributed ten thousand placards to retail owners to be displayed in store windows calling for the return of "living music." Local 802's executive committee proposed more mass meetings and special public concerts, and they launched a newsletter called the *Theater Pit* for the sole purpose of promoting the strike/boycott. Initially there was some confusion over what the union wanted: were they opposed to sound films in principle or did they want to compel theater owners to hire live musicians to play between screenings? In a short article published a week after the rally, the *New York Times* described the union as wanting to "compel picture and other theatres to abandon 'canned' music and reinstate orchestras, bands and vaudeville."

This prompted a letter from Jacob Rosenberg (secretary of Local 802) and Ralph Whitehead (secretary of American Federation of Actors) explaining that the theater drive was not "a fight against 'canned music'" but rather a "fight for re-employment by men displaced not by the machine but by the elimination of orchestras and actors in order to swell profits."

The confusion about the musician's strike was probably shared by moviegoers who were confronted by picketers chanting, "Bring back flesh." But it is also likely that organized labor was not entirely clear about what the musicians were fighting for. Less than a month into the strike, Local 802 leaders noted a "lack of sympathy, understanding and cooperation on the part of large portions of the general public and trade unions." The theater drive committee decided to regroup by focusing their attacks on "block booking"—the big studios' ability to force independent theaters into showing their feature films—as a means to win support from the Independent Theatre Owners Association. According to this strategy, a successful fight against block booking would "necessitate the elimination of certain pictures and [promote] the use of vaudeville." The union believed that by refusing to enter into block-booking arrangements and encouraging independent theater owners to hire vaudeville acts, they could break the monopoly hold of the big studios and theater chains and create jobs for musicians. Those theaters choosing not to go along with the program would then be the target of Local 802 pickets.

The union's theater drive committee came up with other ideas as well. They produced a small pamphlet outlining the musicians' struggle against canned music, planned to persuade radio stations to subsidize live shows as a source of securing new talent, and proposed picketing only one chain of theaters as a way of concentrating their forces. They also formed neighborhood committees to approach theater managers directly and request live music. The last strategy produced some short-lived results. A few managers in Jamaica, Queens, and the Bronx, agreed to hire vaudeville units to provide forty minutes of entertainment for a reasonable price, though this experiment lasted but a few weeks. Loew's Grand Theatre also agreed to stage a vaudeville presentation between reels, but according to the theater management this turned out to be an economic disaster. Local 802 officials protested, insisting that this "failure" was the prearranged result of hiring third-rate talent and manipulating the books to show a loss.

Streamlining and consolidating the theater drive did not solve the problem of mass support. Movie attendance apparently did not waver, and musicians, for the most part, were not fulfilling their obligation to picket. As an incentive, the local began providing carfare and lunch money for unemployed musicians who volunteered for picket duty. These incentives did little to expand the picket lines, which may be partly explained by the increased police presence outside of theaters caused by the operators' bombings.

In addition, the fear of negative public reaction and the mayor's initial reluctance to grant a parade permit led union leaders to postpone plans for a mass march through downtown on November 14. They were able to secure a permit for an automobile parade for the following Saturday, November 21, that would begin on Broadway and 51st street and end at City Hall. Altogether, they organized seventy-eight vehicles, including trucks donated by the Teamsters Union to carry fifteen- to twenty-piece bands. The main purpose of the motor parade was to draw the public's attention to Local 802's campaign and mobilize more support for live music. In the end, however, it garnered very little attention in the press and failed to win substantial numbers of people to their cause. The onlookers were mostly curious weekend shoppers, some of whom might have been headed for a Saturday matinee.

By the end of December it was clear that the theater campaign was in trouble. Not only did the union have difficulty maintaining picket lines, but a few musicians, particularly in Harlem, were brought before Local 802's trial board for crossing picket lines. And during the last five months of 1936 the local failed to achieve a quorum at any of its monthly general membership meetings. Given the shortage of willing activists, the theater committee decided to concentrate their picketing on neighborhood movie houses rather than large Broadway theaters since the latter were "maintained more for publicity to the picture business than profit and the neighborhood theaters would really feel the pressure more."

Picketing continued through the winter months of 1936–37 but remained largely invisible. It did pick up again in March, after Local 802's executive board decided once again to reassess its strategy. After considering and jettisoning a plan for compulsory picketing, the theater drive committee, made up of David Freed, William Feinberg, Harry Suber, and Robert Sterne, voted to continue to vigorously recruit volunteer pickets and to try to solicit more support from organized labor. Besides the inaugural mass meetings, New York labor leaders had been surprisingly silent with regard to the musicians' strike. Although we can only speculate, it is reasonable to assume that the majority of rank-and-file trade unionists in the city, not to mention labor bureaucrats, crossed the AFM picket line on a regular basis in order to catch the latest films. On the other hand, Local 802 was not always visible at labor solidarity events, with the exception of its militant left wing, which regularly participated in the city's united May Day parade.

In order to try and restore "enthusiasm" for the strike, the executive committee decided to recruit pickets on a strictly voluntary basis. Initially, fifteen hundred members signed up for duty at the beginning of March, and many pledged to accept three or four assignments. But once they hit the theaters the numbers fell sharply. Secretary William Feinberg reported that while the rank-and-file volunteers were sincere, "their personal prejudice against picketing won out over their sincerity when the actual time for their picket assignments arrived. . . . Their absence broke up and demoralized picket lines to such an extent that those who did report would sometimes find themselves all alone, and they too would become discouraged and drop out of the Theatre Drive." Members of the theater drive committee also attributed part of the problem to the policy of giving fifty-cent vouchers for each stint on the picket line. The vouchers not only cost the local about fourteen hundred dollars a week, but Feinberg reported that the payments caused attrition because many employed picketers "could not escape the feeling that in taking picket assignments they were not helping the drive so much as they were depriving some unemployed pickets of an additional 50 cent voucher."

The union's inability to sustain picket lines was only part of the problem. Once again, Local 802 leaders had to rethink their entire strategy. Up until the spring of 1937, the union focused its energies on key theaters known for vaudeville and stage presentations before the transition to sound film. Consequently, they ended up picketing/striking six different theater companies at the same time, thus spreading what strength they had too thin. Now they decided to focus on one company, RKO. They chose RKO because it did not have a single vaudeville theater in New York City and because, in the union's view, it actively destroyed live music by taking over leading vaudeville houses and using them exclusively for motion pictures. At the time, RKO operated twenty-eight houses in the city; Local 802 began picketing nineteen of them.

The executive committee also agreed to drop the campaign's demand to bring back vaudeville and instead ask theaters to simply hire orchestras. Noting that "some people like vaudeville—others dislike it," union officials realized that those who disliked it tended to oppose the campaign. The return of theater orchestras to be used in whatever manner management saw fit, they reasoned, should generate a broader base of support. And they were not demanding a band in every theater. On the contrary, in their struggle with RKO the union asked the chain to place orchestras in eight of their twenty-eight theaters, or two orchestras each for Manhattan, Queens, Brooklyn, and the Bronx. If RKO refused to negotiate, the union pledged "to throw the full force of the strength of the local against them."

Infused with new ideas, renewed enthusiasm, and a more manageable agenda, Local 802 launched their RKO campaign at the beginning of April of 1937. Immediately, however, their efforts were stalled by the discovery that RKO employed five organists (Arlo Hultz, Ralph Tishbang, Leo Weber, Bob West, and B. Cowhan) in theaters Local 802 picketed. The union could not continue their actions as long as the organists worked there. Meanwhile, RKO management threatened to fire the organists if the picketing continued. With the approval of national AFM leadership, Local 802 elected to withdraw the musicians and continue picketing, but Hultz, Tishbang, Weber, West, and Cowhan had no intention of giving up their jobs for a campaign that had not yielded any victories in seven months. Worried about their source of livelihood, the organists petitioned the union to allow them to extend their engagement until the upcoming AFM convention in June. When their proposal was rejected, they then asked for strike benefits, to which the executive committee agreed.

The RKO campaign generated more rank-and-file support than any of the previous initiatives since the theater drive was first launched in September of 1936. On June 1, Local 802's executive board met with president Weber to discuss the possibility of turning their citywide struggle into a national campaign, promising to draft a resolution on the matter for the upcoming national convention. Their battle with RKO even showed signs of greater confidence and audacity on the part of Local 802. On June 12, picketers orchestrated a successful sit-in demonstration at the Palace Theater and they felt they had just begun to force RKO management to the negotiating table.

We will never know what might have happened next because a week later, during the AFM national convention in Louisville, Local 802 failed to get national support for their theater drive. In fact, the New York delegates were at the center of a stormy debate over what to do about "canned music." Introducing fifteen specific proposals from the floor to restrict the mechanization of music, Local

802 delegates argued that "the abuse and misuse of mechanical reproduction of music constitute a threat which may annihilate the profession." Weber, on the other hand, vehemently opposed Local 802's proposal, particularly their suggestions for direct action against the studios and a ban on recording. The convention overwhelmingly shot down the local's proposals, including their plan for a national theater drive. The New York delegates left the convention feeling so betrayed by the AFM's national leadership that one Local 802 member, J. F. McMahon, wrote to AFL president William Green criticizing Weber's policies and accusing him of refusing "to assist us in our drive for Live Music." "We must face facts," McMahon continued. "Invention, mass production, and unfettered monster trusts have us by the throat, [but] Weber does nothing."

Without national support, Local 802 leaders believed the movement was doomed. They also concluded that, given what the local had already paid out in strike funds, vouchers, and relief, to continue the drive would amount to financial suicide. So on July 8, 1937, the executive committee of Local 802 voted to end their "strike" against the movie theaters. An inauspicious ending to what had turned out to be a fairly inauspicious campaign.

POSTLUDE: "ALL ABOUT THE BENJAMINS," OR, THE *WORK* OF ART IN THE AGE OF MECHANICAL REPRODUCTION

While the theater campaign turned out to be a dismal failure, it did expose the need for a more thoughtful policy regarding mechanical reproduction and musicians' labor. And despite Weber's initial conservative opposition to the New York delegation, not long after the 1937 convention he seemed to adopt a more militant stance with regard to recorded music.

First, the AFM bureaucracy directed its attention to radio, proposing that the networks increase the size of the staff orchestras employed by their affiliated stations and limit the use of recorded music in their broadcasts. If they did not do this, the union threatened to strike. Weber later hinted that the strike might extend beyond the radio networks to the record industry as well. Among his most controversial proposals was a licensing agreement that would restrict the use of recorded music to businesses that employed musicians, so if an independent radio station had no musicians on its payroll, it therefore could not obtain a license to play recorded music. Not surprisingly, radio industry executives rejected the plan, calling it a secondary boycott and thus a violation of the Sherman Antitrust Act. But they wanted to avoid a strike and were willing to negotiate. In the end the affiliates collectively agreed to spend an additional $1.5 million for live music, and over two hundred affiliates agreed to either hire orchestras or augment the orchestras they already had in their employ. Even the large networks, NBC, CBS, and Mutual, pledged to increase their annual budget for musicians by half a million dollars.

The mere threat of a strike, to which radio executives had to respond, marked a departure from the AFM's earlier strategies under Weber. He now seemed less accommodating and less willing to accept the idea that the march of technology was inevitable. The AFM's position now was that laboring artists ought to have a legitimate voice in production decisions and control over their work, as well as a share in the allocation of profits. And capital had a responsibility to labor to provide employment opportunities. Yet when Weber finally met with studio executives in the film industry in 1938, all of his militancy seemed to evaporate. Perhaps he was sensitive to the fact that the economy had turned downward, the studios were reporting substantial losses, and the U.S. Justice Department had just hit the film industry with an antitrust lawsuit. Whatever the case, Weber met with the Studio Producers' Committee in New York and made a proposal that seemed astonishing both for its conciliatory tone and its impracticality. Hoping to avoid a strike, he offered to lower the wage scale of Hollywood studio musicians in exchange for bringing musicians back to the theaters.

The committee rejected this, Weber's first proposal, outright, arguing that they had gotten rid of musicians in theaters because employing them in those venues was no longer practical—after all, the public came to the theater for films, not concerts. And even if such a thing could be done, it would mean higher admission fees for patrons and there was no evidence that the public would be willing to pay more for the combination of sound movies and live musical performances. But there was yet another, unacknowledged problem with Weber's proposal. Because the federal antitrust suit proposed that the courts divest the movie studios of the theaters they owned, had the committee accepted Weber's demands it all would have been moot if the studios no longer owned theaters in which musicians might play.

Weber's next plan proved far more radical, but the AFM was in no position to make it happen. He proposed a "tax" on all studio films, the proceeds of which would be used to hire unemployed musicians to give free concerts; there would be a nominal fee on each reel, and it would vary according to the size of the theater. Weber believed this scheme could raise between $18 million and $25 million a year. The producers' committee found the proposal laughable, calling it a form of private welfare. The executives insisted that the plight of jobless musicians was not their responsibility; if they needed relief they ought to turn to the government.

At that point the AFM's negotiations with the Studio Producers' Committee came to an abrupt end. The union never exercised the option of calling a strike of the studios because it would have been doomed to failure. There were less than five hundred Hollywood studio musicians, and to ask them to walk out on behalf of some twenty thousand other musicians nationwide was unrealistic, especially in the midst of an economic crisis.

Weber was never able to persuade the film industry to take responsibility for the massive displacement of musicians by technology, but his successor, James Petrillo, adopted an even more aggressive stance toward the music industry's broader corporate structure. Between 1942 and 1944, when virtually every segment of organized labor committed to a no-strike pledge in support of the war effort, the AFM under Petrillo struck the record industry by banning all union members from making records until the record producers agreed to set aside a percentage of royalties to be used to assist unemployed musicians.

The AFM under Petrillo emerged from the war as a power to be reckoned with; Local 802's membership alone increased from nearly sixteen thousand in 1936 to thirty-one thousand in 1948. Petrillo also became a major target of the government's postwar anti-labor backlash. Besides subjecting the union to a number of investigations and hearings, in 1945 Congress passed the Lea Act—better known as the "anti-Petrillo bill"—which banned the union from using "intimidation," including strikes or boycotts, to compel employers in radio to hire more musicians than were needed. In other words, the union could no longer demand the hiring of "standby" orchestras or determine orchestra size. Furthermore, not only did the passage of the Taft-Hartley Act in 1947, banning closed shops, sympathy strikes, and secondary boycotts, weaken the bargaining power of all organized labor, but a provision in the act outlawed the AFM's record royalty fund. Any sort of industry paybacks to unions that did not involve actual services were now deemed illegal under Taft-Hartley. However, when the AFM's recording contracts expired on January 1, 1948, Petrillo called another recording ban. This time the industry was in a strong position, having made and stockpiled many more records than it could release onto the market at once. The ban lasted almost a full year, culminating in a small victory for the AFM. To replace the record royalty fund, the industry agreed to establish a Music Performance Trust Fund that would finance free concerts and pay struggling musicians union scale.

Neither the fund nor the power held by the AFM lasted very long. As technology continued to advance—especially with the proliferation of jukeboxes, the advent of television, and, more recently, the internet (MP3 and Napster)—musicians continued to struggle for gainful employment and the rightful share of the profits generated from their work. And the union's initial argument that recordings are inherently inferior to live music lost some of its bite as developments in studio technology vastly improved sound quality. The ability of sound engineers to alter pitch, edit, and eliminate mistakes have allowed musicians to improve on the "real thing." During the 1970s and 1980s, with the increased use of sophisticated synthesizers and samplers able to electronically reproduce entire orchestras, musicians faced yet another crisis of displacement. Suddenly a keyboard and a programmer could do the work of a seventy-piece band and do it flawlessly. Although musicians were never fully replaced, television and film studios increasingly turned to synthesized music to produce soundtracks.

For musicians, then, perhaps the problem of the twentieth century is the problem of the power line. At the same time, the new technologies have been a source of new creative as well as financial possibilities. Mechanical reproduction has generated opportunities for musicians by making all kinds of music more available to the public and giving many struggling artists access to worldwide distribution. Technological advances have also encouraged experimentation and the creation of new musical genres that utilize recording and playback devices—mixers, digital samplers, turntables, drum machines, computers—as instruments.

The problem, in other words, has never been simply a matter of technology. Rather, the real question is, What should be the relationship between the laboring artist and the market? How much should musicians receive for their labor? What percentage of the current global, multi-trillion-dollar entertainment industry is rightfully theirs? When will we see musicians as workers and realize that wealth in the music industry is generated in the same way it was generated in the coal mines of Ludlow: through the exploitation of creative labor?

Bibliography

THE COLORADO COAL STRIKE, 1913–14

Samuel Yellen's *American Labor Struggles* (Harcourt Brace, 1936) first led me to the Colorado coal strike, which occupies one chapter in that collection of essays on ten important labor conflicts, from the railroad uprisings of 1877 to the longshoremen's strike of 1934 in San Francisco.

Priscilla Long's *Where the Sun Never Shines: A History of America's Bloody Coal Industry* (University of Colorado, 1989) is a beautifully written account that includes the story of the strike and much more, and is indispensable background for the events I describe in this essay.

There is valuable firsthand testimony in the two government reports on the strike. One is the three-volume report of the U.S. Commission on Industrial Relations, *Report and Testimony* (Government Printing Office, 1916). The other is the two-volume report by the House Mines and Mining Committtee, *Conditions in the Coal Mines of Colorado* (Government Printing Office, 1914).

The official summary of the report of the Commission on Industrial Relations is by George West, *Report on the Colorado Strike* (Government Printing Office, 1915).

For descriptions of life in the mining camps, see George Korson, *Coal Dust on the Fiddle* (Folklore, 1965), as well as McAlister Coleman, *Men and Coal* (Farrar & Rinehart, 1943).

Bibliography

Out of Our Depths, by Barron Beshoar, son of the miners' physician, is a biography of John Lawson but also an account of the strike.

Report to the Governor, by Edward Boughton (Denver, 1914), is the report of the military commission set up by Governor Ammons to report to him on the fateful events of April 20, 1914, at Ludlow.

Militarism in Colorado, by William Brewster (Denver, 1914), is the six-hundred-page compilation of reports on National Guard brutality.

The Great Coalfield War, by George McGovern (former senator from South Dakota and presidential candidate) and Leonard Guttridge (Houghton Mifflin, 1972), is the first book-length account of the Colorado strike.

Buried Unsung: Louis Tikas and the Ludlow Massacre, by Zeese Papanikolas (University of Utah Press, 1982), is an extraordinarily vivid piece of research based on many firsthand interviews with participants in the strike.

The only participant's book on the strike is by Mary Thomas O'Neal (described in my essay as Mary Thomas), *Those Damn Foreigners* (Hollywood, 1971).

The mine owners' point of view is presented in *Facts Concerning the Struggle in Colorado for Industrial Freedom,* by the Committee of Coal Mine Managers (Denver, 1914).

There is an excellent biography of Mother Jones by Dale Fetherling, *Mother Jones, The Miners' Angel: A Portrait* (Southern Illinois University Press, 1974).

Philip Foner has edited a fine collection of Mother Jones's speeches and writings, *Mother Jones Speaks* (Monad Press, 1983).

The newspapers and periodicals I consulted for contemporary articles and commentaries are: the *Rocky Mountain News,* the *United Mine Workers Journal,* the *New York Times,* and the *International Socialist Review.*

Bibliography

GIRL STRIKERS OCCUPY CHAIN STORE, WIN BIG

For the history of Woolworth's, start with James Brough, *The Wool-worths* (New York: McGraw-Hill, 1982). See also Robert C. Kirkwood, *The Woolworth Story at Home and Abroad* (New York: Newcomen Society, 1960); John P. Nichols, *Skyline Queen and the Merchant Prince* (New York, Trident Press, 1973); John K. Winkler, *Five and Ten: The Fabulous Life of F. W. Woolworth* (New York: Robert McBride, 1940); *F. W. Woolworth at Ninety: Diversified for Dominance* (Orange, Conn.: Lebhar-Friedman, 1968); Alan R. Raucher, "Dime Store Chains: The Making of Organization Men, 1880–1940," *Business History Review* 65 (spring 1991): 130–63; Adele Hast, ed., *International Directory of Company Histories* (Detroit: St. James Press, 1992, 1998), vol. 5, 224–27; vol. 20, 528–32; Annual Reports, F. W. Woolworth Company, 1912–1950; regular articles in *Chain Store Age* during the 1920s and 1930s.

On Barbara Hutton, the best source is C. David Heymann, *Poor Little Rich Girl: The Life and Legend of Barbara Hutton* (Seacaucus, N.J.: L. Stuart, 1984); see also Brough, *The Woolworths.* Other sources include Dean Jennings, *Barbara Hutton: A Candid Biography* (New York: Frederick Fell, 1968); and Philip Van Renssalaer, *Million Dollar Baby: An Intimate Portrait of Barbara Hutton* (New York: Putnam, 1979). For a wonderful analysis of cosmetics, beautification, and women's appropriation of both, consult Kathy Peiss, *Hope in a Jar: The Making of America's Beauty Culture* (New York: Henry Holt, 1998). For tips, *How to Get Your Man and Hold Him,* illustrated by Dorothy Hoover Downs (A. L. Taylor, 1936), is still widely available in stores that sell used and rare books.

On the growth of chain stores—including additional material on Woolworth's—the literature is vast. A sampling includes Godfrey M. Lebhar, *Chain Stores in America, 1859–1962,* third ed. (New York: Chain Store Publishing Co., 1963); Charles G.

Bibliography

Daughters, *Wells of Discontent: A Study of the Economic, Social, and Political Aspects of the Chain Store* (New York: Newson & Co., 1937); William J. Baxter, *Chain Store Distribution and Management* (New York: Harper & Bros., 1928); John Peter Nichols, *The Chain Store Tells Its Story* (New York: Institute of Distribution, 1940); Raucher, "Dime Store Chains"; Thomas Mahoney and Leonard Sloane, *The Great Merchants: America's Foremost Retail Institutions and the People Who Made Them Great* (New York: Harper & Row, 1966); Joseph Gustaitis, "The Nickel and Dime Empire," *American History* 33, no. 1 (1998): 40–46.

For the anti-chain movement, see Carl G. Ryant, "The Unbroken Chain: Opposition to Chain Stores During the Great Depression" (M.A. thesis, University of Wisconsin, Madison, 1985); Thomas W. Ross, *Store Wars: The Chain Tax Movement,* Working Paper No. 34, University of Chicago Center for the Study of the Economy and the State (July 1984); Thomas Ross, "Store Wars: The Chain Tax Movement," *Journal of Law and Economics* 24 (April 1986): 125–37; F. J. Harper, " 'A New Battle on Evolution': The Anti-chain Store Trade-at-Home Agitation of 1929–1930," *American Studies* 16, no. 3 (1982): 407–26; F. J. Harper, "The Anti-chain Store Movement in the United States, 1927–1940" (Ph.D. dissertation, University of Warwick, Centre for the Study of Social History, 1981). For the chains' reply, see E. C. Buehler, *Debate Handbook on the Chain Store Question* (Warren, Kansas: University of Kansas).

For working conditions and management strategies at Woolworth's in the 1930s, Therese Mitchell's *Consider the Woolworth Workers* (New York: League of Women Shoppers, 1940) provides a gold mine of interviews and information, with information on New York organizing as well. Mary Elizabeth Pidgeon's *Women in 5-and-10-Cent Stores and Limited Price Chain Department Stores* (Washington, D.C.: Government Printing Office, 1930;

Bibliography

U.S. Department of Labor Women's Bureau Bulletin No. 76) offers a national survey of Woolworth's workers; see also Janet Hooks, *Women's Occupations through Seven Decades* (Washington, D.C.: Government Printing Office, 1947; U.S. Department of Labor Women's Bureau Bulletin No. 218). For tidbits on Woolworth's management strategies see also Baxter, *Chain Store Distribution and Management,* and Walter S. Hayward and Percival White, *Chain Stores: Their Management and Operation,* third ed. (New York: McGraw-Hill, 1928).

For the big picture of the CIO in the 1930s, consult Robert Zieger, *The CIO 1935–1955* (Chapel Hill, N.C.: University of North Carolina Press, 1995); Foster Rhea Dulles and Melvyn Dubofsky, *Labor in America: A History,* fourth ed. (Arlington Heights, Ill.: Harlan Davidson, 1984). For the General Motors strike, the definitive study is Sidney Fine's *Sit-Down: The General Motors Strike of 1936–1937* (Ann Arbor: University of Michigan Press, 1969). For the UAW and the strike, see Nelson Lichtenstein, *The Most Dangerous Man in Detroit: Walter Reuther and the Fate of American Labor* (New York: Basic Books, 1995); Henry Kraus, *Heroes of Unwritten Story: The UAW 1934–39* (Urbana, Ill.: University of Illinois Press, 1993); Edward Levinson, *Labor on the March* (New York: Harper & Bros., 1938).

On the Detroit labor movement in 1937, I am indebted to Steve Babson, *Working Detroit: The Making of a Union Town,* with Ron Alpern, Dave Elsila, and John Revitte (New York: Adama Books, 1984); Alpern, Babson, Elsila, and Revitte, *Union Town: A Labor History Guide to Detroit* (Detroit: Workers' Education Local 189); Carlos A. Schwantes, "'We've Got 'Em on the Run, Brothers: The 1937 Non-Automotive Sit Down Strikes in Detroit," *Michigan History,* fall 1992, 179–99.

For an understanding of the AFL and women workers, see Alice Kessler-Harris, *Out to Work: A History of Wage-Earning*

Women in the United States (New York: Oxford, 1982); Dorothy Sue Cobble, *Dishing It Out: Waitresses and Their Unions in the Twentieth Century* (Urbana, Ill.: University of Illinois Press, 1991); Elizabeth Faue, *Community of Suffering and Struggle: Women, Men, and the Labor Movement in Minneapolis, 1915–1945* (Chapel Hill, N.C.: University of North Carolina Press, 1991); Annelise Orleck, *Common Sense and a Little Fire: Women and Working-Class Politics in the United States, 1900–1965* (Chapel Hill, N.C.: University of North Carolina Press, 1995). For the CIO, see Ruth Milkman, *Gender at Work: The Dynamics of Job Segregation by Sex During World War II* (Urbana, Ill.: University of Illinois Press, 1987); Nancy Gabin, *Feminism in the Labor Movement: Women and the United Auto Workers, 1935–1975* (Ithaca, N.Y.: Cornell University Press, 1990); Vicki Ruiz, *Cannery Women, Cannery Lives: Mexican Women, Unionization, and the California Food Processing Industry, 1930–1950* (Albuquerque, N. M.: University of New Mexico Press, 1987); Sharon Hartman Strom, "Challenging 'Woman's Place': Feminism, the Left, and Industrial Unionism in the 1930s," *Feminist Studies* 9 (1983): 359–86. For an analysis of the concept of "girl strikers" and their relationship to consumer culture in an earlier period, see Nan Enstad, "Fashioning Political Identities: Cultural Studies and the Historical Construction of Political Subjects," *American Quarterly* 50, no. 4 (1988).

For the Woolworth's strike itself (including many of the headlines employed in my text), I used, first of all, newspaper and magazine accounts of the time, including the *Detroit News, Detroit Times, Detroit Free Press, Chicago Tribune, New York Times, Daily Worker, Women's Wear Daily*, and *Life*. A spectacular set of photographs of the strike is available in the *Detroit News* Collection, Archives of Labor and Urban Affairs, Walter Reuther Library, Wayne State University, Detroit. Two newsreels produced by Pathé News are available through the Grinberg Film Library in New York City. The *Detroit Labor News,* collected in the Archives of Labor and Urban Affairs, Walter Reuther Library, Wayne State University, Detroit, covered the upsurge in Detroit labor activity before, during, and after the strike. Candy Landers of HERE Local 24 (formerly Local 705) generously allowed me to use the local's private papers, including the *Michigan Hotel, Bar, and Restaurant Review,* scrapbooks, and Floyd Loew's invaluable correspondence. I was able to find membership lists and a variety of background materials on microfilm at the international offices of HERE in Washington, D.C.

I also found material on the strike in *Catering Industry Employee,* HERE's magazine, and in *Retail Clerks International Advocate,* both of which are important sources on their respective unions' activities in 1937. For background, consult especially Cobble, *Dishing It Out;* Matthew Josephson, *Union House, Union Bar: A History of the Hotel and Restaurant Employees and Bartenders International Union, AFL-CIO* (New York: Random House, 1956); and George C. Kirstein, *Stores and Unions: A Story of the Growth of Unionism in Dry Goods and Department Stores.* National statistics on the CIO are from Leo Troy, *Trade Union Membership, 1897–1962* (New York: National Bureau of Economic Research, 1995).

For Myra Wolfgang/Mira Komaroff, see Jean Maddern Pitrone, *Myra: The Life and Times of Myra Wolfgang, Trade-Union Leader* (Wyandotte, Mich.: Calibre Books, 1980); Bernard Rosenberg and Saul Weinman, "Young Women Who Work: An Interview with Myra Wolfgang," *Dissent* 19, no. 1 (winter 1972): 29–36; and extensive clippings, resumés, and correspondence in the papers of Local 24, which also provided material on Louis Koenig.

For solidarity with Detroit workers on the part of the retail clerks' union in New York City, as well as its own activities, see materials in the Robert F. Wagner Archives, New York University, including interviews with Clarina Michelson and May Brooks and files on retail clerks' organizing. The Library of Congress collection of the *New York World Telegram and Sun* contains photographs of the New York Woolworth's strike, filed under "Labor-Retail" and "Labor-Strikes." *The Retail Employee,* from the New York local that split off from the Retail Clerks' International Protective Association, also reports on organizing activities. For New York union organizing and the national ripple effects of the Detroit strike, see Kirstein, *Stores and Unions,* and the *Retail Clerks International Advocate* throughout 1937 and 1938.

Finally, on the popular culture front, "Chain Store Daisy" is from Harold Rome's *Pins and Needles* (New York: Florence Music, 1937). For text and an analysis of its context, see Michael Denning, *The Cultural Front: The Labor of American Culture in the Twentieth Century* (London and New York: Verso, 1996). *The Devil and Miss Jones* (Republic Entertainment, 1941) is available on video through Republic Entertainment, Inc.

WITHOUT A SONG

Primary Sources

The main sources for this essay include the records of Local 802 of the American Federation of Musicians, housed on microfilm at the Tamiment Library, New York University. The "Minutes of the Executive Board" and "Minutes of Regular Membership Meetings" were especially useful for reconstructing the events before and during the theater campaign.

The following bibliography lists periodicals, documents, and handbooks that were essential for reconstructing the transition to sound as well as the strike itself:

Periodicals: *Billboard, Down Beat, Film Daily, International Musician, Metronome, Modern Music, Moving Picture World, New York Amsterdam News, New York Herald Tribune, New York*

Bibliography

Sun, *New York Times*, *Theatre Pit* (temporary newsletter of Local 802), and *Variety*.

Associated Musicians of Greater New York. *Price List Governing Special and Regular Engagements of the Associated Musicians of Greater New York, American Federation of Musicians.* Newark: 1936.

Associated Musicians of Greater New York. *Price List Governing Single and Steady Engagements of Electrical Transcriptions, Movie-Tone, Opera, Radio, Recordings, Symphony, Theatres and Wired Music of the Associated Musicians of Greater New York: Local 802, American Federation of Musicians, In Effect September 15th, 1939.* Newark: 1939.

"Effect of 'Talking Movies' Upon Employment of Musicians and of Actors," *Monthly Labor Review* 27, no. 5 (November 1928): 159–60.

"Effects of Technological Changes Upon Employment in the Motion-Picture Theaters of Washington, D.C.," *Monthly Labor Review* 33, no. 5 (November 1931): 1–14.

Frelinger, Gregg A. *Motion Picture Piano Music: Descriptive Music to Fit the Action, Character or Scene of Moving Pictures.* Lafayette, Ind.: Gregg A. Frelinger, 1909.

Kiesling, Barrett C. *Talking Pictures: How They Are Made, How to Appreciate Them.* Richmond, Va.: Johnson Publishing Co., 1937.

Kisseloff, Jeff, ed. *You Must Remember This: An Oral History of Manhattan from the 1890s to World War II.* San Diego: Harcourt Brace Jovanovich, 1989.

Lang, Edith, and George West. *Musical Accompaniment of Moving Pictures: A Practical Manual for Pianists and Organists.* New York: Arno Press, 1970 reprint (orig. 1920). First issued by the Boston Music Company.

Robinson, Earl, with Eric A. Gordon. *Ballad of an American: The Autobiography of Earl Robinson.* Lanham, Md. and London: Scarecrow Press, Inc., 1998.

Bibliography

Sabaneev, Leonid. *Music for the Films: A Handbook for Composers and Conductors,* trans. by S. W. Pring. London: Sir Isaac Pitman & Sons, Ltd., 1935.

U.S. Congress, Committee on Education and Labor. *Restrictive Union Practices of the American Federation of Musicians,* vol. 1. Washington, D.C.: Government Printing Office, 1948.

U.S. Congress, House Committee on Education and Labor. *Special Subcommittee to Investigate James C. Petrillo, the American Federation of Musicians, et al.* Washington, D.C.: Government Printing Office, 1947.

Secondary Sources

Anderson, Gillian B. (comp.). *Music for Silent Films (1894–1929): A Guide.* Washington, D.C.: Government Printing Office, 1988.

Austin, Mary. "The American Federation of Musicians' Recording Ban, 1942–1944, and Its Effect on Radio Broadcasting in the United States." M.S. thesis, North Texas State University, 1980.

Benjamin, Walter. "The Work of Art in the Age of Mechanical Reproduction," in *Illuminations,* trans. by Harry Zohn. London: Pimlico, 1999.

Bogle, Donald. *Toms, Coons, Mulattoes, Mammies, and Bucks: An Interpretive History of Blacks in American Film.* New York: Continuum, 1989 (new ed.).

Braverman, Harry. *Labor and Monopoly Capital: The Degradation of Work in the Twentieth Century.* New York: Monthly Review Press, 1974.

Burlingame, Jon. *For the Record: The Struggle and Ultimate Political Rise of American Recording Musicians within the Labor Movement.* Hollywood, Calif.: RMA Recording Musicians Association, 1997.

Chanan, Michael. *Repeated Takes: A Short History of Recording and Its Effects on Music.* London: Verso, 1995.

Commons, John R. *Types of American Labor Unions: The Musi-*

cians of St. Louis and New York. N. P.: 1906. (Pamphlet reprinted from *Quarterly Journal of Economics* 20 [May 1906]).

Countryman, Vern L. "The Organized Musicians," *University of Chicago Law Review* (autumn 1948 and winter 1948).

Crafton, Donald. *The Talkies: American Cinema's Transition to Sound, 1926–1931.* New York: Charles Scribner's Sons, 1997.

Cullen, Jim. *The Art of Democracy: A Concise History of Popular Culture in the United States.* New York: Monthly Review Press, 1996.

Denning, Michael. *The Cultural Front: The Laboring of American Culture in the Twentieth Century.* London: Verso, 1996.

Dickerson, Lowell Dwight. "Central Avenue Meets Hollywood: The Amalgamation of the Black and White Musicians' Unions in Los Angeles." Ph.D. diss., University of California, Los Angeles, 1998.

Doherty, Thomas. "This Is Where We Came In: The Audible Screen and the Voluble Audience of Early Sound Cinema," in Stokes and Maltby, *American Movie Audiences,* pp. 143–63.

Edwards, Richard. *Contested Terrain: The Transformation of the Workplace in the Twentieth Century.* New York: Basic Books, 1979.

Erenberg, Lewis A. *Steppin' Out: New York Nightlife and the Transformation of American Culture, 1890–1930.* Chicago: University of Chicago Press, 1981.

Everly, Philip K. *Music in the Air: America's Changing Tastes in Popular Music, 1920–1980.* New York: Hastings House, 1982.

Eyman, Scott. *The Speed of Sound: Hollywood and the Talkie Revolution, 1926–1930.* New York: Simon and Schuster, 1997.

Flinn, Caryl. *Strains of Utopia: Gender, Nostalgia, and Hollywood Film Music.* Princeton: Princeton University Press, 1992.

Gomery, Douglas. *Shared Pleasures: A History of Movie Presentation in the United States.* Madison: University of Wisconsin Press, 1992.

Griffiths, Alison, and James Lathan, "Film and Ethnic Identity in

Bibliography

Harlem, 1896–1915," in Stokes and Maltby, *American Movie Audiences,* pp. 46–63.

Handy, D. Antoinette. *Black Women in American Bands and Orchestras,* 2nd ed. Lanham, Md. and London: Scarecrow Press, Inc., 1998.

Hansen, Miriam. *Babel and Babylon: Spectatorship in American Silent Film.* Cambridge, Mass.: Harvard University Press, 1991.

Johnson, James Weldon. *Black Manhattan.* New York: Arno Press, 1968, orig. 1930.

Jowett, Garth. *Film: The Democratic Art.* Boston: Little, Brown, 1976.

Kennedy, Michael, ed., *The Oxford Dictionary of Music,* 2nd ed. New York: Oxford University Press, 1994.

Kraft, James P. *Stage to Studio: Musicians and the Sound Revolution, 1890–1950.* Baltimore and London: Johns Hopkins University Press, 1996.

Kubach, John Scott. "Unemployment and the American Federation of Musicians: A Case Study of the Economic Ramifications of Technological Innovations and Concomitant Governmental Policies Relative to the Instrumental Employment Opportunities of the Organized Professional Musicians." M.A. thesis, Ohio University, 1957.

Lens, Sidney. *Labor Wars: From the Molly Maguires to the Sitdowns.* Garden City, N.Y.: Anchor, 1973.

Leonard, Neil. *Jazz and White Americans: The Acceptance of a New Art Form.* Chicago: University of Chicago Press, 1962.

Levine, Lawrence W. *The Unpredictable Past: Explorations in American Cultural History.* New York: Oxford University Press, 1993.

Lewis, David Levering. *When Harlem Was in Vogue.* New York: Alfred A. Knopf, 1981.

Lipsitz, George. *A Rainbow at Midnight: Labor and Culture in the 1940s.* Urbana: University of Illinois Press, 1994.

Loft, Abram. "Musicians, Guild, and Union: A Consideration of the

Evolution of Protective Organization among Musicians." Ph.D. diss., Columbia University, 1950.

Marks, Martin Miller. *Music and the Silent Film: Contexts and Case Studies, 1895–1924.* New York: Oxford University Press, 1997.

May, Larry. *Screening Out the Past: The Birth of Mass Culture and the Motion Picture Industry.* New York: Oxford University Press, 1980.

Mazzola, Sandy R. "When Music Is Labor: Chicago Bands and Orchestras and the Origins of the Chicago Federation of Musicians, 1880–1902." Ph.D. diss., Northern Illinois University, 1985.

McChesney, Robert. *Telecommunications, Mass Media, and Democracy: The Battle for Control of U.S. Broadcasting, 1928–1935.* New York: Oxford University Press, 1993.

Milazzo, Christopher. "A Swan Song for Live Music?: Problems Facing the American Federation of Musicians in the Technological Age," *Hofstra Labor Law Journal* 13 (spring 1996): 557–81.

Montgomery, David. *Workers Control in America: Studies in the History of Work, Technology and Labor Struggles.* New York: Cambridge University Press, 1979.

Musser, Charles. *The Emergence of Cinema: The American Screen to 1907.* New York: Scribner's, 1990.

Nasaw, David. *Going Out: The Rise and Fall of Public Amusements.* New York: Basic Books, 1993.

Ogren, Kathy J. *The Jazz Revolution: Twenties America and the Meaning of Jazz.* New York: Oxford University Press, 1989.

Oja, Carol J. *Making Music Modern: New York in the 1920s.* New York: Oxford University Press, 2000.

Osofsky, Gilbert. *Harlem: The Making of a Ghetto: Negro New York, 1890–1930.* New York: Harper and Row, 1963.

Prendergrast, Roy. *Film Music: A Neglected Art.* New York: Norton, 1991.

Refior, Everett Lee. "The American Federation of Musicians: Organization, Policies, and Practices." M.A. thesis, University of Chicago, 1955.

Reuss, Richard A. *American Folk Music and Left-Wing Politics, 1927–1957.* Lanham, Md.: Scarecrow Press, 2000.

Ross, Steven J. *Working-Class Hollywood: Silent Film and the Shaping of Class in America.* Princeton: Princeton University Press, 1998.

Seltzer, George. *Music Matters: The Performer and the American Federation of Musicians.* Metuchen, N.J. and London: Scarecrow Press, 1989.

Sklar, Robert. *Movie-Made America: A Cultural History of American Movies.* New York: Random House, 1975.

Sklar, Robert, and Charles Musser, eds., *Resisting Images: Radical Perspectives on Film History.* Philadelphia: Temple University Press, 1990.

Smulyan, Susan. *Selling Radio: The Commercialization of American Broadcasting, 1920–1934.* Washington, D.C.: Smithsonian Institution Press, 1994.

Spivey, Donald. *Union and the Black Musicians: The Narrative of William Everett Samuels and Chicago Local 208.* New York: University Press of America, 1984.

Stokes, Melvyn, and Richard Maltby, eds. *American Movie Audiences: From the Turn of the Century to the Early Sound Era.* London: British Film Institute, 1999.

Stowe, David W. *Swing Changes: Big Band Jazz in New Deal America.* Cambridge, Mass.: Harvard University Press, 1994.

Thissen, Judith. "Jewish Immigrant Audiences in New York City, 1905–1914," in Stokes and Maltby, *American Movie Audiences.*

Wolff, Catherine. "Labor Relations in Symphony and Opera Orchestras." M.A. thesis, American University, 1982.

Acknowledgments

HOWARD ZINN

I must thank Deborah Chasman of Beacon Press, who approached me with the brilliant idea for a book on Three Strikes, which would be neither about baseball nor about California's absurd criminal law. And special thanks to Chris Kochansky for editing the manuscript with her usual keen intelligence.

DANA FRANK

A great array of people helped me track down sources, understand Detroit in the 1930s, and find people to interview, and I want to thank them all, beginning with Eric Abrahamson, Ron Alpern, Alberta Asmer, Steve Babson, Irwin Bauer, Paul Buhle, Carolyn Davis, Michael Denning, Sean Ellis, Peter Gottlieb, Douglas Haller, Darran Hendricks, Desma Holcomb, Mildred Jeffreys, Bill Mazey, Harry Miller, Kathy Moran, Keith Phelps, Franklin Rosemont, Ethel Schwartz, and Ferrer Valle. Thanks especially to Paul Domeney, Mary Davis, and Ceil McDougle, for their stories of the strike itself and of working at Woolworth's. Thanks to Michael Rogin for sharing his own work on *The Devil and Miss Jones*. My great thanks, as always, to David Montgomery, for help with sources and ongoing inspiration.

I am especially indebted to the Hotel Employees and Restaurant Employees' International Union (HERE) for so generously— and with such enjoyable comradeship—opening its archives to me,

Acknowledgments

both in Washington, D.C., and in Detroit. Thanks to the people who made it possible: Rick Faith, Pat Lamborn, Candy Landers, Morty Miller, Lee Strieb, and John Wilhelm.

Too late, I want to thank Debra Bernhardt, to whose memory this book is dedicated. Debra was a spectacular fighter for labor history who for almost twenty years guided me to sources in the Wagner Archives at New York University—including all the materials here on retail clerks in New York. Thanks also to the staff of the Wagner Archives; to the staff of the Walter Reuther Library, Wayne State University, especially Tom Featherstone; and to the Grinberg Film Library. I was able to visit all these archives thanks to funding from the UCSC Academic Senate Committee on Research. My astounded thanks, still, to Frank Gravier for tracking down the Pathé Newsreels.

On the home front (and beyond), my deepest thanks to the Usual Suspects for all their support: Barbara Bair, Frank Bardacke, Cathy Buller, Nancy Chen, Sami Chen, Joan Couse, Gerri Dayharsh, Eleanor Engstrand, Julie Greene, Lisbeth Haas, Hamsa Heinrich, Ramona Dayharsh McCabe, Rebecca Dayharsh McCabe, Steve McCabe, Gwendolyn Mink, Amy Newell, Mary Beth Pudup, Gerda Ray, Karin Stallard, Tyler Stovall and Deborah Turner. Thanks to my family—Carolyn, Joseph, and Laura Frank—for their ongoing love and support. (Thanks especially to my mom for finding me an actual Detroit Woolworth's worker, at the San Luis Obispo, California, League of Women Voters.) My particular thanks to the friends who read the manuscript and helped it along with enthusiasm and advice: Miriam Frank (no relation!), Marge Frantz, Desma Holcomb, Ann E. Kingsolver, Greta Schiller, Debbie Shayne, Vanessa Tait, and Andrea Weiss. My special thanks, once again, to Nelson Lichtenstein for his ongoing enthusiasm for my work, for his expertise on Detroit in the 1930s, and for his gracious humor about my pilgrimage to UAW-centrism. Special thanks to Carter Wilson for comradeship in writing, for oh-so-

Acknowledgments

smart advice on the manuscript, and, most important, for enduring (half) the TV movie with Farrah Fawcett as Barbara Hutton.

Thanks, finally, to Robin D. G. Kelley and Howard Zinn for the enormous honor of sharing their marquee, and for the great pleasure of working with them. Thanks to Edna Chiang at Beacon Press for support during the hard parts, and to all the Beacon folks. And, most of all, thanks to Deborah Chasman, who thought up the book and invited me in; who once again gave me great advice; and who was always supportive, savvy, and fun along the way—the editor all writers dream of.

ROBIN D. G. KELLEY

First and foremost, thanks to the incomparable Deb Chasman for birthing the idea of this book in the first place and for her patience as I floundered and hesitated in the initial stages of production, and to Tisha Hooks for reminding me that floundering can be a good thing. Much gratitude to my coauthors, for their patience and especially for their imagination—without which I would not have been able to tell the story I told. Of course, to Diedra and Elleza, for their love, humor, and tolerance for my most recent musical experiments. Diedra read and commented on earlier drafts; her enthusiasm made me excited about the work all over again. Thanks to Patricia Cooper and Julie Greene, I had the pleasure of presenting an early draft of my essay as the keynote address to the Labor and Working Class History Association. All of the participants—too many to mention here—gave me critical advice, for which I am immensely grateful. Peter Rachleff, Betsy Esch, and Vijay Prashad, in particular, helped me rethink several crucial political questions, and many conversations with graduate students proved very valuable in sharpening my analysis. Finally, I must thank the entire staff at the Tamiment Library, especially Andrew Lee and the late Debra Bernhardt, who passed unexpectedly and prematurely during the course of my research. I would not have figured out the American

[173]

Acknowledgments

Federation of Musicians without Debra's selfless guidance. She was one of the great labor archivists and a committed movement person who, on the eve of her death, was desperately trying to build up primary source collections for the history of black labor in New York State. It is to her that I dedicate this book.